Enneagram

Your Personality Type and Path to Self-discovery
and Self-development

(Basic Guide to Enneagram and Spirituality)

Theodore Fahey

Published by Knowledge Icons

Theodore Fahey

All Rights Reserved

Enneagram: Your Personality Type and Path to Self-discovery and Self-development (Basic Guide to Enneagram and Spirituality)

ISBN 978-1-990084-60-7

Legal & Disclaimer

The information contained in this book is not designed to replace or take the place of any form of medicine or professional medical advice. The information in this book has been provided for educational and entertainment purposes only.

The information contained in this book has been compiled from sources deemed reliable, and it is accurate to the best of the Author's knowledge; however, the Author cannot guarantee its accuracy and validity and cannot be held liable for any errors or omissions. Changes are periodically made to this book. You must consult your doctor or get professional medical advice before using any of the suggested remedies, techniques, or information in this book.

Table of Contents

Introduction

The goal of every person on earth today, is to become the truest, highest and best version of themselves. Even though career, social, and background paths may differ, this is the ultimate need of man. Some experts prefer to call this, "self-actualization."

The fact is that if you don't know who is, then how in the world are you going to become the best version of yourself? To actualize yourself, you must first discover yourself. When you discover yourself, the knowledge of your discovery will open doors for you to begin certain actions, steps and strategies that will commence the transformation process to become whom you aspire to be.

The Enneagram of Personality is an ancient tool that has set many people on the path of self-actualization. Due to the incredible impact, it has become very useful and popular in recent times. Many psychologists, life coaches, priests, spiritual leaders, therapists, and counselors have been using it to help their clients discover themselves and improve their life.

The Enneagram offers an exciting and thrilling way to start the process of self-discovery, and then take the necessary actions to develop ourselves. It is no wonder that the self-discovery tool has gained global popularity and has transformed the lives of millions of people across the globe.

By understanding the Enneagram and learning how to use it to improve your life, you will catapult yourself into the next level of progress in your life. Not only will you see changes in your life, but the progress that will be made will help you gain a deeper knowledge of yourself, maximize your potential and become the best of yourself.

The Enneagram classifies personality into nine types. Each human being has a core type and accompanying wing type. Each of personality has its own strengths and weaknesses. Through an Enneagram test, you can find your type and know your blind spots. The insight gleaned will also set you on track to develop yourself and maximize your potential. The following entails nine personalities of the Enneagram:

Type One—The Reformer/Perfectionist

Type Two—The Helper/Giver

Type Three—The Achiever/Performer

Type Four—The Individualist/Romantic

Type Five—The Investigator/Thinker

Type Six—The Loyalist/Skeptic

Type Seven—The Enthusiast/Epicure

Type Eight—The Challenger/Boss

Type Nine—The Peacemaker/Mediator

Discovering your Enneagram type does not only help you but also the people around you. It changes the way you relate with others. When you discover your type and begin to work on yourself, you gain a deep sense of self-awareness which helps to connect better with other people. This opens doors for you to empower yourself to form a strong relationship with others.

You learn to accept other people, as opposed to criticizing them. Instead of exhibiting the deadly sins of each your enneatype, you exhibit the healthy virtues. As Jim Rohn said, "Success is something you attract by the person you become." As you discover and work on your personality type, you develop an attractive personality that people like and trust.

In the following pages and chapters, you will discover how the Enneagram can change and transform your life forever. From discovering your Enneagram type, finding balance by developing a healthy personality and applying the wisdom of the Enneagram to all areas of your life, you will find exciting tips, advices, and strategies to take your life to the next level. Enjoy your reading!

Chapter 1: The Sacred Enneagram:

Historical Origins

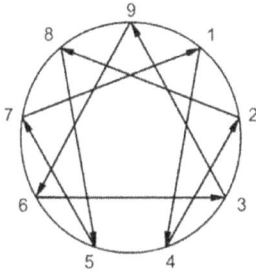

The history of the Enneagram of Personality is widely disputed, but there are some main points that are agreed upon as major contributing factors. There certainly seem to be roots that can seem be traced back at to the philosophy of Ancient Greece. Some will emphasize the mathematical and geometrical qualities and evoke Pythagoras and Boethius; others point to its connections to the tradition of Kabbalah. These various traditions make up the framework that expresses the intrinsic archetypes that can be found in the Enneagram of Personality, and serve as perspectives and traditions to consider when approaching the use of the Enneagram for self-development. The Enneagram's ancient history provides the basis for its relevance with Christianity; many of these sources had been influences on Christian thinking from the very beginning.

Platonic Essentialism serves as a founding for many of the archetypes and symbolic systematology involved in the foundations of the Enneagram. Basically, this comes from the philosophy of Aristotle and Plato and, it states that every person has an "essence." This "essentialism" is a core human concept that alludes to the Essence of the soul, and it was germinated in Greece and Asia Minor. Eventually the ideas moved, as spices and materials did, geologically south, to areas now known as Syria and even further to Egypt. It was in these places that the ideas were adopted by early Christian mystics who focused on the ways that the divine form was lost in the ego. This is the origin of the Christian concept of the seven deadly sins. The original inspiration for the Christian seven deadly sins was contained by the same material that contained the nine types in the Enneagram.

Most scholars agree that it was the Sufis, people from sect of Islam that emphasizes mysticism and ecstasy, who developed the concept of personality types. They were a spiritual and mystical people, who did a lot of work in the area of spiritual research. The Sufis' culture was deeply ingrained with mysticism. It was under their influence in the 14th and 15th centuries that the idea of personalities become defined. It was a Sufi belief that there were nine essential patterns or orientations to life. These patterns and orientations represented the image of God that exists within that person. There is also the other side of this representation: the opposite force within the person, which serves to block the realization of the power within.

The Sufis had a tradition of spiritual development that encouraged people to find their way to God over many years, and they witnessed from direct observation the nine ways in which peoples' personalities manifest, and how they run in to obstacles in their journey. To condense the Sufi's primary question, one could put it like this: What happens? What happens to our original goodness? What happens along the way to cause us to be distracted, or anxious, or too angry to have clarity in our lives?

The Sufis' believed that our psychological and spiritual development – our experiences, our upbringing, our attitudes and positioning in the world – grow a tension between two dualistic truths that are available to each aspect of us: the virtue, or essential truth that mimics the divine form, or the vice, which serves to distort and subvert each virtue.

Think about the way that our upbringing and context influences the way our personality is expressed. If a child grows up in a chaotic household, an environment in which she must protect herself, then she will develop ways to protect herself. The most developed and often used parts of the child's personality will be the ones that serve as protection. This could manifest itself in many ways, whether the strategies are good for the child or not. Once these behaviors and attitudes are firmly established, a person feels like they have an identity, and the ego starts to take hold. We then develop strategies to protect the undeveloped parts from criticism.

The Sufis had a beautiful long tradition of meditation and prayer and mysticism. This path toward spiritual guidance led the Sufis to integrate many concepts with spirituality. As their mathematical capabilities grew in the fifteenth century, Sufi mathematicians discovered the decimal system. This led to the concept of periodic decimal fractions (when one is divided by three or seven). As their scientific and mathematical understanding of the world grew, this knowledge was incorporated and fused into their spiritual understanding, and the Enneagram was one of the products of this marriage of science and faith. In the nine points of energy that the Enneagram describes, the Sufis saw nine refractions of the one divine love. The word enneagram itself comes from the Greek words ennea (nine) and gramma (letter).

The Sufis' understood the potential for insight in exploring our vices. The Sufi tradition asks "What do our negative qualities teach us?" and it encourages the idea that positive and enriching value can be gleaned from exploring our negative sides. Before we can move on and understand ourselves, we have to look at how we are benefitting from the vices.

Kabbalah is a mystical ancient strain of Judaism. It is at once a school of thought, a method, and a discipline of Judaism. It contains the Tree of Life. The Tree of Life is a symbol in Kabbalah that is said to be a map illustrating various aspects of the world and our experience in it. The Tree of

Life offers another interpretation of the divine forms which are manifested in our behaviors. The Kabbalah has nine Sefirot, which correlate with the Enneagram. Point One aligns with Hochma (all knowing, correct, internalized father, Abba), Point Two with Bina (understanding, controlling, supernal mother, ima,) Point Tree with Gedula (impetus to be great) Point Four with Tiferet (beauty, romantic longing, point five with Din (bound, enclosed, limited) Point Six with nezeh (enduring seeking authority), point seven with Hod (splendor), Point Eight with Yeysod (seminal force) and point nine with shechina (accepting presence).

Because of its wide-reaching, possibly universal roots, the enneagram seems to be mostly congruent with most major religious traditions. The enneagram is known in the Christian tradition to be a bridge between spirituality and psychology. With some research, we can see how the system of the Enneagram fits in with multiple secular and sacred sources regarding vices and virtue, or intelligences

11

and weaknesses. Multiple ancient personality systems are contained in variants of the Enneagram model in Christianity, Sufism and Judaism implies that the Enneagram has an ancient and common resonance with may peoples of earth. In the table below, four ideological interpretations are made of concepts contained in the Enneagram.

Enneagram	Kabbalah	Capital Sins	DSM-V
1.) The Perfectionist	Hochma – All knowing, correct	Anger	Compulsive
2.) The Giver	Bina- Understanding, supernal mother	Pride	Histrionic
3.) The	Gedula –	Deceit	Narcissis

Performer	Impetus to be great	(self)	t (secondary)
4.) The Romantic	Tiferet - beauty, romantic longing	Envy	Depressive
5.) The Investigator	Din-Bound, enclosed	Avarice	Avoidant
6.) The Loyalist	Nezeh-seeking authority	Fear	Paranoid
7.) The Enthusiast	Hod--splendor	Gluttony	Narcissist (primary)
8.) The Protector	Yesod-Seminal force	Lust	Sociopath
9.) The Peacemaker	Shecihina-accepting presence	Sloth	Obsessive-compulsi

			ve

Ivonovich Gurdjeff has a significant place in the history of the Enneagram. He was a Russian adventurer and seeker who had studied Tibetan, Sufi, Indian and Christian mysticism. Interestingly, Gurdjieff became aware of the enneagram in Afghanistan. Gurdjieff didn't use the enneagram as typology of personality, however. He saw it as a sort of philosopher's stone, which had deep resonance in the archetypal experience of humanity. Gurdjieff's enneagram seems to have come somewhat directly from the Kabbalistic Tree of Life. Gurdjieff's studies laid the foundation for Oscar Ichaz0's work.

 The most modern significant phase of the development of theory around the Enneagram was in the 1960's and 70's, during the work of philosopher Oscar Ichazo. Ichazo was native to South America, and after visiting various parts of Asia, he returned to Buenos Aires to develop his ideas, and eventually created the Arica School. The Arica School consisted of a system of psychology influenced by metaphysics and spirituality, based on the centuries of enrichment around the Enneagram symbol, created to help people reach new levels of self-realization. Ichazo's new conception of the Enneagram acknowledges influence of mystical Judaism, Christianity, Islam, Buddhism, and ancient Greek Philosophy. He saw his work as a way to make clear the relationship between our essential selves and our ego-selves; to Ichazo, there is a potential in each human to be at harmony with the world, to be thriving against its challenges and settling in when there its comfort and ease.

The Enneagram is a topology; it is not unique in this, and there are various other systems of typology for personality. Astrology, for example, finds twelve categories for types. Psychologist Carl Jung, in his writings, uses the premise that there are three pairs of functions that are expressed differently in each person: extroversion-introversions, perception-intuition, and thinking-feeling. In each case, a person will favor one of each, leaving us with eight distinct personality types. Jung's archetypes also support and enrich the Enneagram. Jung's archetypes and how they relate to the types of the Enneagram will be discussed later.

The Myers'-Briggs typology is one that has been widely used since its conception. Isabel Briggs Myers developed this system by considering a different set of functions. Those are judging-perceiving, the inclination to quick, clear judgments and decisions as opposed to receptivity to many influences and kinds of information. She eventually developed the Myers-Briggs Type Indicator, a test that distinguishes among the sixteen types that are present there.

The psychoanalyst Fritz Riemann was influenced by astrology when he worked out a scheme of human fears. He assumes four basic human fears: the fear of nearness, fear of distance, fear of change, and fear of permanence. This results in

Riemann's four basic types: Schizoid, depressive, compulsive, and hysterical.

The guiding principle for all of these different models of personality classification is that all people are different, but that some individuals have experiences and behaviors and attitudes that are remarkably similar. to one another. A typology can be thought of as a sort of map, that has the purpose of facilitating and overview of the soul. The Enneagram is a circle whose circumference is broken up by nine points. The points are numbered clockwise from 1 to 0. Points 3, 6, and 9 are bound together in a triangle, as are 1, 4, 2, 8, and 5, and 7 in a hexagon.

Chapter 2: The Absolute Beginner's Guide

To The Enneagram Of Personality

So in the Enneagram, you are an absolute beginner... You heard how incredible and helpful it could be, but you're not sure what's the big thing... Now, if you want the basics of the Enneagram, pull a seat up and continue reading.

Before I proceed, I would like to say that there are various ways to understand what we are aware of the Enneagram. There are several different "schools of thinking" on this subject, which you will definitely discover when you delve into it. Having said that, what you're reading will be jaded, reflective, just slightly educated, but hopefully enough to sample the Enneagram. More importantly, you are pushing for deeper digging.

Literally, the Enneagram is a symbol. It is a nine-pointed symbol that has appeared over the past few decades in many religions. No one knows how the ancients conducted the study or how they used it until very recently. Enneagram Spectrum sums up the speculations of the origins of the Enneagram thus: "The roots of the Enneagram are controversial. Some authors believe that variations on the Symbol of the Enneagram in the sacred geometry of the Pythagoreans, who 4000 years ago were interested in the meaning and meaning of numbers, have been found. Ichazo, I think, was the first person to actually apply the enneagram laws to the nine laws functioning in the human psyche.

Today's way of understanding the Enneagram is that it is a tool that helps people to understand and formulate nine "filters" for the world. Such filters are complex, subjective, and may or may not actually exist, but they can lead to dramatic realizations in relationships and personal growth with the aid of resources.

I think it's a great way to understand how to liken these filters to the "operating systems" of computers. Many people run Windows, some of them run Linux, some of them use an Apple computer. They are all different ways of taking, arranging, and reacting to the sensory input.

The beauty of this study is that you gain a viewpoint that you have not seen before when you can express the most profound feelings and experiences of your family, dear ones, and particularly yourself. You simply see yourself. Like never before...

The Enneagram is carried in many different directions by different schools. Some offer advice on how to succeed professionally, and some provide Life Coaches with information to help their customers. Others drive you to your limits by discovering the places you can use to form. And many schools do much more outside of the scope of this Complete Beginner's Guide. You're there to explore, enjoy, and comment on.

Enneagram - Are You Sure of Your Type? Are You Mis-Typed?

In the analysis of the modern Enneagram, one of the main concerns is mistyping. You probably know somebody who typed on a book or website, and you may not agree with the decision. And as difficult as it is to hear, we type many of us on the basis of who we hope or think we are, rather than how we really are.

This guide is meant to help you confirm your type, or for the first time to discover your type, avoiding the common pitfalls associated with self-type.

Without delay, here's the...

7 When finding (or confirming) your type, things to consider: 1. Until you dive into typing, ensure that you have a basic understanding of each form.

Just as you must understand the basics of how a car functions before you decide whether it is the brakes or the radiator, you must know the nine types before you can know your own type with certainty.

2. Take the Enneagram Exam for free.

There are a couple of tests that will try to find your type online. Although they are not unfailing, they are definitely part of the process. I won't recommend one in particular, but you can find one that fits your needs on Google's "Enneagram Test."

3. Address the test questions honestly.

Make sure that you don't respond to how you think of yourself or want to be! It is so easy to do this, but you can only get the Enneagram value if you get the right type. So be honest! So be honest!

4. Recall that all types are the same.

Sometimes people hear that they are a four and wonder if it's less than one or half an 8. The numbers are signs only. All kinds are special, equal, interesting, lovely, and have something to offer. Enjoy your man! Love your woman!

5. Find your wing. Find your wing.

Every form of Enneagram has a wing. In your form, wings can make a big difference. Even though not everyone agrees about the wing's validity, I consider it valid more than false, so I still recommend it. Your wing can be one of the two numbers adjacent to your form number sequentially. For example, type 3 could have a 2 or 4 wing. It would be written 3w2 or 3w4 like this. A type 6 could have a five wing or a seven wing. See the pattern? See the pattern?

To find your wing, under your type number, I'd look at Enneagram site and find the wing section and see which one seems to fit you most. The wings are typically much easier than your form to decode.

6. Mind you might not see your guy in yourself too clearly.

It is very difficult to see ourselves critically. You may not see the components of your Enneagram type right away, so it is important to do step 7...

7. Find an Enneagram study group, student, or practitioner to confirm your findings and to help you take the next step.

Find a local Enneagram group that can be called or attended by a meeting. It is very convenient for somebody to hang out with you for a few hours and, after a few talks, let them know if you have found the right number. The kind of someone who practices and studies the Enneagram for a while is a lot about his "energy" and has improved his purpose. Therefore, most teachers think that the Enneagram's "oral tradition" is the only way to pass the legacy. So if you are genuinely interested, the most powerful tool you can have is to have a group of friends and a community to learn from!

The round-up: Finding your type is just the beginning of your journey through this wonderful tool, the Enneagram. Make sure you find the right guy and have done a great favor to yourself. Live well, love lots, and continue to grow.

Power of Enneagram for Personal Growth and Relationships

Relationships are an important part of our daily lives. The relationship you have with your parents loved ones, friends, and even you play a key role in your sense of happiness and personal success.

This is how Enneagram's power comes as a helpful tool for opening the secret door for people of true understanding... And connecting on a deeper level with ourselves and others.

Have you ever done something that left you confused afterward when you were upset or hurt? Or you watched the unusual and different acts of a loved one... And why do you have no clue?

It's natural for years to live with someone... And in them, we don't know yet hidden depths and corners. What can we really expect? We've been living with us for a lifetime... But we don't really learn our entire inner side.

Thanks to the power of Enneagram, you will discover for the first time ever-not only why you are, but also the most effective tool for seeing and decoding people's actions. It is truly a lovely gift to understand why everyone works the way they do and reaches the core of their hearts.

As one wise friend has always said, "The greatest need for us is to understand and be understood because this provides us with true, unconditional love and acceptance."

Here are just three ways to learn more about Enneagram's personal and business partnership tips:

1. You're a truly unique human being, and you know yourself, your strength, and your weak points. With your energy and presence, the gifts you bring to this world every day are a magical combination of strengths and weaknesses. We both have-whether we embrace or run away. We all have both.

And the strongest and most intelligent people are those who adopt their abilities and follow their inner call, also know their dark side and learn to live with it in peace. Thus the Enneagram helps you touch both sides and develop from both sides.

You don't have to hide or run from your fears or shortcomings in a perfect world. You should embrace your inner self-with everything it offers. That's when you're at best. And the Enneagram helps you with this specifically.

2. We are social beings around you, sure. We are social beings. We benefit by being surrounded and connected with the people we love. When you press with someone else's inner voice... Sparks fly. Sparks fly. And that moment of comprehension and communication is really priceless, isn't it?

But it doesn't happen so often now, isn't it?

It seems to happen only once in a blue moon when we genuinely and deeply interact with another human. If you really feel like you share the same vision, energy, and passion-so to speak.

So what if I told you that every day could happen? What if you could see through the guards and masks of men... And see in them the pure inner child? What if, after 5 minutes, you could skip the little talk and have a strong connection with a stranger?

Would it not be amazing to go through such a day?

It would really be. And the good news is that it is entirely possible. It was a mighty journey after five years of working with the Enneagram to finally be able to grasp loved ones.

In the following guides, you will find out more about how you can develop this power soon. Stay tuned! Stay tuned!

3. Have you ever felt out of place at work or between a group of friends? Find your unique path towards development and ultimate happiness? Have you felt that you didn't belong in your gut? But anyway, you silenced the speech because it was meaningless?

Maybe if you could find the place where you really feel at home for the first time ever?

What if you have the tools to find out what you really want? The profession that gives life to your passion...

The relationship you feel at home with...

Everything is possible with Enneagram... And so much more. And so much more.

When you discover a unique type of Enneagram, you can see how vibrant your inner calling is as the Sun is and how you can improve your relationships at home and at work.

Chapter 3: Your Enneagram Personality (9 Types)

A few years ago I went to a therapist in Philadelphia. I was in need of some help getting back on my feet after ending a crappy relationship and figured a licensed therapist was a good place to start. I goggled some in the area and found one that sounded like a great fit.

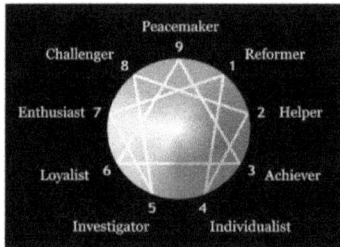

Having never been to a therapist before, I thought it would be like the movies: a sofa, a box of tissues, and a therapist asking tearprovoking, "and how did that make you feel" type questions. To my surprise, my first visit was not like that at all. Before we even got to the reason I was there, she asked if I wanted to take a "Personality Inventory". I told her I had no idea what she was talking about, but yes! I do (I love to try new things). She explained it was called the "Enneagram" (pronounced any-a-gram) and that the test for it would consist of a long list with pairs of statements, and I was to choose the one that sounded "most like me". She said I should pick the statement that speaks more to who I am as an adult (not as I was as a child) and that the statements were not necessarily opposing.

I couldn't wait to take the test. I rushed home and after about an hour and a half of reading and choosing between pairs of statements, I calculated my score and the test revealed that I am a Type 7: "The Enthusiast". I read the short description of the 7 (there were 9 personality descriptions) on the back of test and I was amazed at how much I could relate to it. Constantly seeking new experiences? Yes. Impatient and impulsive? Yes and yes!

Desires feeling content and fulfilled, afraid of being deprived and in pain? Oh my gosh, yes! How could a few short sentences sum up my inner thoughts, behaviors and feelings?

After a few more visits with the therapist, a few books ordered on amazon, and goggling the "Enneagram" too many times to count, I was totally hooked. Type 1, that's my mom. Type 5 sounds like my dad. Type 8, totally my sister. Type 9, yes, that's my brother! The descriptions were so accurate. As a "typical" seven (loves to share experiences with others, gets overly enthusiastic about things!!!), I told everyone who would listen about the Enneagram. So if you'll listen too, here it goes...

All humans have what is known as a personality, which the American Psychological Association defines as our "individual differences in characteristic patterns of thinking, feeling, and behaving."

Over the centuries, various philosophers, psychologists, schools of thought and the like have broken our understanding of these differences down further into personality types and disorders, which are further explained by groups of distinct personality traits, each of which explains the way we handle everything and anything from criticism, self-care, romantic relationships, friendships, family, vulnerability, energy, and so on.

The Enneagram system is one such means of classification, which, according to the Enneagram Institute, "can be seen as a set of nine distinct personality types, with each number on the Enneagram denoting one type."

Those who study this system believe that each of us "emerges from childhood with one of the nine types dominating their personality, with inborn temperament and other pre-natal factors being the main determinants of our type ... by the time children are four or five years old, their consciousness has developed sufficiently to have a separate sense of self. Although their identity is still very fluid, at this age children begin to establish themselves and find ways of fitting into the world on their own."

Moving into adulthood without having recognized the basis of your own unique personality, limits your potential in life, as you will not be able to survive without your ego.

The Enneagram, thankfully, serves to help you find your personal passion and purpose in life by, among other things, helping you become aware of unhelpful habits and patterns you love out unconsciously, but which no longer serve you.

Thankfully, you have, right within you, the wisdom to discover your passion and purpose in life, and the Enneagram can help you unlock the wisdom that is already there.

Is one type more likely to be successful under particular circumstances than another? The answer is both "Yes" and "No."

Each type brings specific skills, which are the gifts that come quickly to you. However, if you get to a place where you can be healthy in most of the nine types, there is no limit to what you can do.

Your goal should be becoming as self-observant as you can, watching out for old patterns that surface in times of stress.

Your personality alone is not your true self, and by using the Enneagram the discover more about your passions and potential, you can achieve and be at your best self.

As you read through the list of nine types below, pay attention to you instinctive center (located in your belly), the emotional center (located in your heart), and the thinking center (located in your head). When you are able to stay present with who you are, you will know what you need to be about.

Read on to discover who you, your purpose, and your passions really are, according to the traits of the nine Enneagram of personality types:

THE PERFECTIONIST

You know there is a better way to live life and you have a passion for making the world a better place. You often are intuitive and have a strong connection to the unknowable that connects us all.

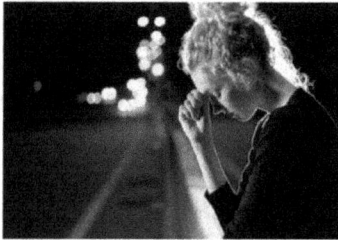

Learn how to notice your inner critic, that loud negative voice that tries to prevent you from doing things that you have never done before. This negative voice can prevent you from having new experiences out of your ego's need to keep you safe. You are now an adult and are most capable of taking care of yourself.

Watch out for the times when you become fearful of not doing your job correctly. It is okay not to do everything exactly right. If you are too focused on perfection, you may miss opportunities to have new experiences. New experiences can lead to finding your purpose or passions in life.

When you are well, you will be able to hear the inner voice of your soul. The sound of your true self is gentle and quiet and you'll learn how to notice the difference between this voice and the voice of the inner critic. It will let you know when you have found your purpose and passion. You will know it when you see it.

This personality type is also called the Reformer. Their underlying motivation is anger. They pursue perfection in life and when it doesn't happen, they often get angry and then very anxious. They are extremely loyal people with high moral values who work very hard to protect and look after their family and loved ones.

People of this personality type are essentially looking to make things better, as they think nothing is ever quite good enough. This makes them perfectionists who desire to reform and improve; idealists who strive to make order out of the omnipresent chaos.

They have many positive qualities. They have an excellent eye for detail for example. In effect, they will dot all the letters 'I' and cross all the letters 'T' in everything they do. Driven by a harsh inner critic, they always try very hard to make sure everything they do is as perfect as it can be. This triggers their need to improve, which can be beneficial for all concerned, but which can also prove to be burdensome to both the type 1 and those who are on the receiving end of the type 1's reform efforts.

But they also have negative qualities. They can be very quick to judge other people although they feel very guilty doing so. Despite their obvious gifts, they often cannot appreciate their own value and tend to struggle with their inner critic - the voice inside their head telling them how useless they are. They tend to believe that others are just being nice when they give them a compliment.

Ones have a fine eye for detail. They are always aware of the flaws in themselves, others and the situations in which they find themselves. This triggers their need to improve, which can be beneficial for all concerned, but which can also prove to be burdensome to both the One and those who are on the receiving end of the One's reform efforts.

The One's inability to achieve the perfection they desire feeds their feelings of guilt for having fallen short, and fuels their incipient anger against an imperfect world. Ones, however, tend to feel guilty about their anger. Anger is a "bad" emotion, and Ones strive sincerely and wholeheartedly to be "good." Anger is therefore vigorously repressed from consciousness, bursting forth in occasional fits of temper, but usually manifesting in one of its many less obvious permutations - impatience, frustration, annoyance, and judgmental criticality. For this reason, Ones can be difficult to live with, but, on the high side, they tend to be loyal, responsible and capable partners and friends.

Ones are serious people; they tend to be highly principled, competent and uncompromising. They follow the rules and expect others to do so as well. Because they believe so thoroughly in their convictions, they are often excellent leaders who can inspire those who follow them with their own vision of excellence. Reform movements are frequently spearheaded by Ones.

Ones are often driven and ambitious, and are sometimes workaholics. But whatever their professional involvement, they are definitely active, practical people who get things done. They are natural born organizers, list makers who finish everything on the list, the last one to leave the office, the first one to return, industrious, reliable, honest and dutiful.

The relentlessness of their pursuit of the ideal can make Ones tense people who have a hard time relaxing and who unnecessarily deny themselves many of the harmless pleasures of life. They tend to be emotionally repressed and uncomfortable with expressing tender feelings; they generally see emotionality as a sign of weakness and lack of control. They are seldom spontaneous. They have multiple interests and talents however; they are self-reliant and seldom run out of things to do.

Ones are often intelligent and independent and can easily mistake themselves for Fives, but unlike Fives, Ones are primarily people of action, not thought. Ones tend to worry and are prone to anxiety and can sometimes mistype as Sixes, but they are far less affiliative than Sixes and their standards are not reached by seeking consensus with a group. Finally, the relentless pursuit of perfection can take its toll and lead to depression. At such times, a One can mistype as a Four. But Fours have a tendency towards self-indulgence whereas Ones are self-denying. Fours are emotionally expressive; Ones are emotionally constrained

Ones are a body-based type with an emphasis on personal integrity and self-control. Their attention goes toward seeing and correcting what is wrong, and doing the right thing. They are known for their honesty, dependability and common sense.

Ones are very responsible, so much so that they may resent other people who don't take life as seriously as they do. They have high standards and tend to see things in black and white, right and wrong. It's easy for them to be critical, of themselves and others. They work hard at being right all the time. They are idealistic and will exert great effort to improve the world around them, which often puts them in the role of social reformer. Their crucial elements of growth are to learn to accept their imperfections and tolerate other people's points of view.

Strengths

Reformers have some great strength. They will usually be great students and meticulous employees. These are the employees and students that acquaint themselves with the rules and regulations from their first day and won't forget them as long as they are there. Type 1s would be extremely unlikely to break the rules in any setting, unless they were asked to do something that conflicted with their morals. Reformers will uphold the values and standards of any school or workplace to the letter. This Enneagram type is often particularly drawn to religion because of its rules, morals and guidelines. They will feel particularly secure if these rules are in written form, and may often go back to look at them frequently to reassure themselves.

Doing the right thing is very important to this type. They are great at self-development in this respect, as they can change their behavior to fit in with new morals and standards.

Another big plus with this type is their love for justice. Law-breakers and those who hurt others engage them. If they can channel this anger into productivity, you will probably find them campaigning, organizing and trying to make a difference.

Neurotic Style

However, this love of morals comes with some downsides. When they approach life situations, the first thing that comes to their mind is rules, values, and 'right' or 'wrong'. This means that they can come across as quite judgmental about the behavior of others. They may miss the nuances of a situation because they are thinking in such a black and white way. This leads to them being perceived as insensitive, because they often don't take the time to try and understand other people's feelings and emotions. For them, it is not relevant to know the reasons behind why someone has done something 'wrong'. To them, it is just 'wrong' and no amount of explanation can justify or mitigate it.

Type 1s are likely to criticize people, which can lead to strained relationships. If they get quite set in their ways, Type 1s can feel building resentment towards those who don't see the world in the way that they do. Those with different morals are branded as 'wrong', and their reluctance to change their ways to the Reformer's standards make Type 1s angry. They are likely to form a view of other such people as 'corrupt' and 'bad people', and it may be very difficult to change their mind on this. They can also suffer from massive shock and feelings of betrayal when someone they admired does something they see as 'bad'.

Unintentional hypocrisy can also be a problem for Type 1s. Their reaction to what they perceive to be 'bad' can be so extreme that they exhibit the very behavior they condemn. For example, a Type 1 would know that cruelty is wrong.

However, if they feel very strongly that someone else has made an error, they might act in a cruel way towards that person. They are so focused on the deed of the other person that they forget their own deed in the process, and may act out in ways they would judge other people for. If Type 1s recognize this hypocrisy on their part, they are deeply ashamed. They are likely to be very disappointed that they behaved in this way and violated their morals, and will beat themselves up mentally for much longer than is called for. They will worry that they are a bad person and put themselves down.

Morality

Luckily, the Type 1s have a great gift in their morality. They are unlikely to be law breakers and will try their best to live upright and productive lives. A great self-development opportunity for a Reformer is to try to understand other people's inner lives and why they do the things they do. If we can withhold judgment for long enough to learn about their struggles in a compassionate way, we get deeper beneath the good/bad aspect and really get to know the person. Someone who can uphold their own morals and show understanding to others can be a huge inspiration for others to follow and improve themselves. A way Type 1s can soothe their anger and frustration is to focus on the concept of 'Essence'. This means looking beyond someone's behavior and into their essential being. Some religions and traditions would call essence 'soul' or 'spirit'. If we can try to imagine what it feels like to be another person and how they experience life, we can gain compassion for them.

With the virtues of morality and understanding, Reformers are in prime position to make changes for the better in our world. When they have made time for self-development in their lives, they bring a sense of justice to everything they do and can be a source of constant inspiration to those around them. They will be steadfast and courageous leaders of the highest moral caliber when they work for personal growth.

- Iman Mohiki

Strengths: Honest, responsible, and improvement-oriented

Problems: Resentful, non-adaptable, and overly critical

Speaking style: Precise and detail-oriented, with a tendency to sermonize

Lower emotional habit: Resentment, which results from getting angry but holding it in

Higher emotion: Serenity, which comes with letting go of anger about the way things are and accepting imperfection

Archetypal challenge: To change what can be changed, to accept what cannot be changed, and to develop the wisdom to know the difference

Psychological defenses: Ones use the defense mechanism of reaction formation to avoid their anger (and other feelings and impulses) and maintain the self-image of being "right." (Reaction formation is feeling one thing and then doing the opposite, such as feeling resentful but acting nice).

Somatic patterns: As body-based types, Ones are usually grounded and practical, good at ordering the tasks of daily life. The pressure to be right and the need for control leads to physical rigidity and tension, particularly in the jaw, neck, and shoulders. The face can take on an expression of angry judgment or resentful martyrdom.

Following study and evaluation of yourself, you can learn to manage these negatives so that your personality will attach itself to the positive characteristics of your type. Being hard working, direct when appropriate and attempting to change the world for the benefit of others are your positive qualities and these will be naturally highlighted when you learn to control the negatives.

Chapter 4: Types Of Enneagram And How To Recognize And Use Your Type To Improve Your Relationship

This chapter will discuss how enneagram can improve your relationship with your partner and aid your personal and mental growth. After reading this chapter, you are expected to know how to use the enneagram of personality to make your relationship a beautiful one. It is expected of you to know how you can use it to develop your mental state and advance your personal and professional growth in an unprecedented manner. It is also expected of you to be able to tell you the type of enneagram and the type you would love to be. The Enneagram system has profound depth and nearly predictable accuracy that can be said to be unmatched. Enneagram works as a perfect tool that helps us to differentiate 9 separate different personality groups and what exactly drives their behaviors and attitudes. For leaders, managers, the whole team and the entire organization, enneagram of personality allows human beings to amplify their chances of success by getting the needed primary understanding of the deep motivations that dictate each and every person's behaviors, thought patterns, emotions, and worldviews.

For several years, in fact, more than ten years now, I have been using Enneagram in every gathering I am invited to speak about individual differences, dissimilarity and how we can have harmony in diversity. I have also used it in every symposium, seminars workshops just to help the political leaders and many multinational organizations further discover their personal and professional success in a way that is somehow unprecedented. All the people I have had cause to relate with or work with has given me some feedback on how the Enneagram of Personality has significantly and tremendously impacted how they perceive of themselves and other people in their life.

Regardless of anything, each of us is programmed in a unique way that is slightly and at the same time, tremendously different from that of the next fellow. By identifying our personality group and that of our colleagues in the grand scheme of the Enneagram of Personality test we can quickly become more aware of the way through we react to situations, issues, and environment. By that, we will become exposed to things that will enable us to achieve our ultimate intentions and desired outcomes, and we will be able to overcome our most dreaded fears. Being aware of things close to us is the key to a growth mindset which we must have if we are to help our relationship grow as we would love it to grow.

Once you successfully acquire growth of mindset, then you can excel in your relationships, you can have more than twenty of years of a relationship in one year of fraternizing period with your partners, co-worker or lover.

How the Enneagram of Personality makes your relationship grow

Before we go further, you must continuously remind yourself that the Enneagram symbol or image represents different shades of personalities.

You must also remember that the word Enneagram has its etymology in Greek with "ennea" standing for nine and "gram," whether written or drawn standing for diagram. Essentially, enneagram is a kind of personality system that has nine personality groups arranged in an orderly manner around the exterior of a circle just as the way it can be seen on the cover of this. The nine types are neatly arranged in a clockwise manner around the outside of the diagram. Each one of the personalities has an arrow pointing away from it and another arrow pointing towards it distinctly. These arrows show the transitions that occur when each type is either at a disadvantage or at an advantage. For Enneagram group one, for instance, if you look closely you can see that the arrow that is relatively pointing towards it from the Type or group seven. This shows that when Group one is relaxed and under no duress or stress, they take on the beneficial aspects of the type or group seven. Inversely, the arrow that points away from the group one is also pointing toward group four, which means they take on the advantages and beneficial aspects of group four when under stress or duress. What is notable here is that both act in one particular way or the other when they are healthy or stressed. What I want you to understand is that for your relationship to function well and work out, you need to understand the type or group that you belong to and you need to understand that of the other person.

The Nine Identified Enneagram Personalities that can be used to foster your relationship.

These are the personalities identified by Ichazo and some other scholars:

The Reformer (Conscientious and Ethical)

The Helper (Supportive and Sincere)

The Achiever (Self-Assured and Charismatic)

The Individualist (Self-Aware and Reserved)

The Investigator (Alert and Curious)

The Loyalist (Committed and Reliable)

The Enthusiast (Enthusiastic and Spontaneous)

The Challenger (Confident and Controlling)

The Peacemaker (they are calm and too believing)

As an individual, the fact is that your nuances will be formed by all the personality groups' traits, but you will also definitely have one main personality that is prevalent and quite observable in you. In a relationship, you might see these nine types as nine distinct rules which must be duly observed and followed before you can eventually have it your ways. Each of the nine rules has its own subsets, and there are particular ways of reacting to issues through which you can lead others you are in relationship with to a better place. By becoming familiar with each of the rules guiding relationships, you can check your blind spots and recognize the behavioral patterns in other people.

As it was said by Drew Houston who is the CEO of Dropbox app, that the Enneagram is a precious system that every man must have if they are to move forward in their relationship. He maintained that he uses enneagram to make perfect his relationship with other people. Although it was super skeptical at the beginning, he said the practice of enneagram help to boost his relationship and it was like the wave of ocean, and it was so hypnotizing in some ways. Nonetheless, he maintained that enneagram was so helpful in boosting his relationship both individually and with the members of his team because he was able to learn more about them. The enneagram also helped him to identify his blind spots and remove them. He was able to know that he belongs to Enneagram group seven. To him, it was like a manual that gives him what he needs to know to have a lasting relationship and workable affairs with his partners, it helps him to consolidate his friendship, widening his networks. He was able to identify his strengths and weaknesses which is of group 7. He was, through enneagram, able to know that the group or type seven of enneagram of personality likes the novel idea and new things that have never been revealed to anyone. He was also able to know that they are comfortable in chaos, but also that they can easily become unreliable, petty and distracted if all things are not as planned. Through the enneagram of personality, he was able to know why he was so avoidant of chaos and conflicts. One way or another, you must always want and strive for perfections and must look for ways through which you can get a very accurate map that can guide you to having the life that you always wanted and make your relationship work and make you understand ourselves better.

Chapter 5: Type Three– The Achiever

Type Threes are success-oriented and practical. They are driven and adapt to the situation as needed so they can excel in everything they do. Threes are concerned with how people perceive them. They want others to see them as competent to get the job done.

Threes are self-assured and ambitious. However, they also have a charming sense of energy. They are highly driven for advancement in their positions. Threes are poised and diplomatic. They want to make every aspect of their life a success and a model for others.

Healthy Threes are more than capable of achieving great things to change the world. People look up to them because of their accomplishments and their graciousness. Healthy Threes feel good developing and contributing their abilities to those around them. They enjoy motivating others to work hard and see how much they can accomplish.

These are your typical workaholics and competitors. To other people, they may be considered the "teacher's pet" or a "brown-noser." They can be seen going out of their way to stay over at work and skipping breaks to get a job done. They work extremely well under pressure.

Their basic desire to feel worthwhile and valuable can instill a fear of being worthless. Threes may become so consumed with other people's definition of success they lose sight of who they really are. They pursue success for other people rather than personal gain.

Threes perceive emotions as a roadblock to success. Being in tune with their own desires might make them lose respect from others. Therefore, they box up their feelings and interests, in an attempt to appear successful. This need to drown their feelings is usually fueled by their childhood.

They were pressured to believe they were nobody and worthless unless they excelled in certain areas. Many people receive the same type of message, but Threes really take it to heart the most. When confronted with the question, "What do I personally want from life?" They generally do not have an answer because they were never allowed to explore their own interests.

Threes with a Two-wing may be classified as "The Charmer," while Threes with a Four-wing are classified as "The Professional."

Threes have a strong need for affirmation and rewards. They expect acknowledgement of their achievements and may feel used and undervalued when they are not acknowledged for their work.

Stress Point

When Type Threes are stressed, they may exhibit negative or unhealthy levels of development typically seen in Type Nine personalities.

These unhealthy traits include:

Withdrawn

Numb

Stubborn

Neglectful

"Peace at any cost"

Tune out reality

Idealize others

Security Point

During times of growth Type Threes may exhibit positive or healthy levels of development typically seen in Type Six personalities.

These healthy traits include:

Independent

Cooperative

Endearing

Responsible

Hard-working

Persevering

Levels of Development

Healthy:

Level 1

Self-accepting

Threes are authentically modest, charitable, gentle, and benevolent toward helping others. They are full of heart and humor others by putting themselves down.

Level 2

Self-assured

Threes have high self-esteem and know how competent they are. They have confidence in their self-worth. They are charming and gracious. Others desire them because they adapt well to any situation.

Level 3

Ambitious

Threes will do anything to improve themselves into becoming the "best them." They are outstanding role models, and others become motivated to mirror them in positive ways.

Average:

Level 4

High performance

Threes are terrified of failing. They strive for excellence and success. Their self-worth diminishes if they aren't the best.

Level 5

Image-conscious

At this stage, Threes are fully concerned with their reputation and how others perceive them. They begin to lose touch with their feelings and ideas.

Level 6

Narcissistic

They may exaggerate their accomplishments and embellish their strengths. At this point, they become arrogant in their attempt to seek attention and acknowledgment.

Unhealthy:

Level 7

Manipulative

They envy the success others and are willing to fudge ethics to gain an edge. They may lie and cheat to gain promotions.

Level 8

Devious

Unhealthy Threes will become malicious towards others. They will sabotage other people's chance for success.

Level 9

Vindictive

They become relentless in ruining other's happiness. They become obsessed with destroying evidence of their failures.

Chapter 6: The Individualist

Synopsis

"I am me. There is nobody else like me." This is the cry of a nonconformist – one who is distinctive and particular from the rest (as per them...)

This part discusses:

• What a maverick is about

• Why are maverick respect have around

• What is most troublesome about individualists

• Dealing with them and drawing out the best

• Who they coexist with

• Who they don't alongside

Elitist of society, they are continually endeavoring to be remarkable and distinctive. Understanding them requires exertion, yet will yield their special mix of humankind. Simply absolutely never remind them how "regular" they are.

What Is An Individualist?

Themed as 'specials', the maverick is an individual who flourishes as being totally one of a kind to whatever is left of humankind. They are exceptionally reluctant about their singularity and are creatures of unlimited imagination on the grounds that they are unique in relation to others.

Profound scholars and analyzers, they are the logicians of life and they have a solid enthusiasm for expressions, regardless of the possibility that they don't end up to end up specialists.

They are tastefully delicate and they adore everything about elucidation toward oneself, exposure toward oneself or divulgence toward oneself... regularly imparting their awesome discoveries to others and giving a solid commitment to the world.

The Good

Since they see themselves as naturally novel, they are regularly individuals who have a tendency to think out about the case.

They want to come back to the sacred thought of birthplace – regularly diving deep down into themselves to discover the genuine "source" and offer that level of mankind with other individuals.

They are frequently exceptionally cool or reasonable individuals – giving a balance of restraint as they handle circumstances.

Their most effective characteristic is that they esteem uniqueness, recognizing the irregularity found in others and are creatures endeavoring to be as real and valid as could be allowed. You can simply rely on them to express their actual emotions without wearing a veil.

The Bad

A nonconformist typically has a solid propensity to be an elitist – disturbed by the regularity of the masses, they can get to be staggeringly bigot, bias and eager towards contrasts, particularly when it debilitates their uniqueness and thoughts.

They are additionally loaded with jealousy – particularly of things that they need so profoundly that separates them from the rest.

At the point when things happen in life for a nonconformist, they get to be hyper-investigative, regularly falling into profound episodes of sadness and trouble. Withdrawal from the world and self-incurred discipline (just about bordering to the point of masochism...) helps them to feel normal.

Instructions to Deal With Them

Managing an independent is basic. Since they esteem their uniqueness so profoundly that they frequently see it as a gift or a condemnation, it is alright to give them a chance to flounder in dejection for a little while on the grounds that they are candidly intricate and exceptionally touchy.

A self protecting independent must be managed tenderly. Since their uniqueness is never imparted to whatever remains of the world, one must figure out how to endure their inclination to wind up self-ingested in profound thought until they are prepared to turn out and live their lives.

A sexual independent aches to impart their credible and remarkable self to their accomplices – regularly failing enormously when they are in (or after) a contention with their friends and family. In the event that they are confronting discouraging, note that it is critical not to yank them out of their shell on the grounds that it will just further disappoint their dejection.

Social individualists adores common imparting and they want to impart themselves legitimately to substantial gatherings whom they feel that they are standoffish their regularity. On the off chance that things happen, they will regularly withdraw themselves seeing the world as unfeeling and long for a friend in need to come and salvage them.

By the day's end, profound enthusiastic comprehension is imperative on the grounds that all sub-sorts of the maverick long to be comprehended and acknowledged for who they really are.

They discover solace with reformers (sort 1) whose transforming ways issues them a channel that they can channel their special and remarkable ways and they detest being around aides (sort 2) who most likely don't comprehend their uniqueness and detests owing them a feeling of privilege (preferring withdrawal in depression).

Chapter 7: The Enneagram Personality

Types Myths And Facts

In order to get the most out of knowing your Enneagram personality type, you have to stop believing in some common myths that circulate around. The existence of these misconceptions is parallel to the lack of reliable information. When you can't find accurate and reliable information, sources that you do find seem legit. However, believing in these myths prevent you from truly understanding Enneagram, yourself, and other people. That's why the primary objective of this chapter is to focus on the most common myths and their (in)accuracy.

The Enneagram tests don't really work and they are unreliable.

The belief that Enneagram personality tests don't work stems from disagreeing with a description of your type. However, just because you disagree with something it doesn't mean it's wrong. The point of Enneagram isn't to identify good or bad personality types, but to point out your characteristics, strengths, and weaknesses in order to improve self-discovery and perception of the world. In order to get the most reliable results, follow the advice provided earlier in the book (sign up for a workshop, get guidance from someone with more experience, do it online). When it comes to the internet, the best tests are generally not free, but you shouldn't discard them immediately, it's not like you'll do them every day.

Your personality type is easiest to detect when you're very young.

This isn't entirely correct and the reason is simple – your personality is relatively fluid when younger than 21 or 22. Even though you have one dominant personality type and may exhibit characteristics associated with others from time to time, it's easier to detect your type in mid- or late-twenties than earlier in your life. Don't pay too much attention to your age in order to identify whether you're too young /old to identify your personality type. What matters the most is to understand your internal patterns of behavior, thinking, or feeling and answer test questions honestly.

Sixes tend to misidentify themselves as Fours. So, if your personality type is Four, it means you're actually Six.

Personality types Six and Four have some similar characteristics and it is not uncommon for people to mistake them for one another. In fact, chances are higher than someone will mistake you for a Six (if you're Four) than you doing it yourself. Although both types of personality have big similarities, they also have important differences. The point here is to avoid thinking "well this type also applies to me, so that must be it" and acknowledge your dominant type.

You can tell someone's personality type based on the way they handle an argument.

A person's personality type has a lot to do with the way they act in different situations, including arguments, but it's not the best way to determine whether they're One or Nine. Different people perceive some situations differently, so it would be difficult to define a person's personality type during an argument if you're not familiar with their inner patterns. Also, people act differently in various argument settings. For example, you don't act the same way when engaging in an argument online and in your workplace.

Ones are inflexible neat freaks.

If you've researched Enneagram already you've probably come across theories about all personality types. A common theory is that Type One is a neat freak and an inflexible individual due to perfectionist nature. Of course, you'll definitely come across Ones that do fit that role, but it doesn't mean all of them are. It all comes down to the person's belief in what is right or wrong and their vision of the perfect way to get something done. Therefore, if a person believes that flexibility is the key to solve some problem, then that's what they will do.

Twos are extremely needy.

A person who is Type Two is usually perceived needy due to their generous nature that sometimes makes them forget about their own needs. They also want to be irreplaceable. However, these things don't mean a person is overly needy. Always look at the positive side and acknowledge their kindness.

Threes care only about themselves and their own goals.

Even though every Performer wants to achieve the goals he or she has set out for themselves, it doesn't mean they don't care about other people. In fact, their positive attitude in most cases serves as motivation to others so they can accomplish their goals too.

Chapter 8: Outline

An agent is an analyzer of data and the best approach. They are likewise a sort of mastermind who preferences to take a secondary lounge, watch the circumstance, make all the logical contemplations for the best choices and returns after a full examination of the circumstance is finished.

A sort six is a blended sack of apprehension versus mettle, dedication versus distrust and the watchman blessed messenger or the renegade. They are the individual who is embodied by the celebrated melody "Remain by me".

Eyewitness, Investigator,

Mastermind, Sage or Voyeur

They commonly don't impart their enthusiastic state to others as they keep down frequently discovering security in their psyches where they can withdraw and strategize, just to rise later with full certainty! You can simply depend on them to give savvy answers, and when they are keen on something, they have a tendency to end up truly well perused and educated around there.

They are likewise somewhat modest yet more free (or hesitant to acknowledge help) wanting to accomplish things all alone actually when other individuals are more than willing to give help. They tend not to impart anything much particularly when their essential obsession of miserliness is showed.

Their blessed thought is Omniscience. They won't stop until they know and comprehend everything their limited personalities can hold.

Their biggest apprehension is pointlessness or powerlessness. They, in the same way as the sort threes additionally yearning to be profoundly skillful.

They yearning to be skilled in all assignments. Since they are the enormous brains of the gathering, they are frequently looked upon as the one with all the answers and the best approach.

Their greatest allurement is over considering. On account of their contemplative, diagnostic nature, they have a tendency to keep down, not making a move.

Their most noteworthy bad habit is insatiability – due to their longing to know and have everything coupled with their closefisted nature, they regularly fall into this issue of needing everything for themselves. Then again, the sort ones are taking care of business when they figure out how to disengage themselves and live free.

Sort fives with a wing of four and wins of six have one solid qualification – craftsmanship and science. Wing fours consolidate intelligent and enthusiastic creative ability. Those with wings of sixes are actually skilled and are great at discovering the qualifications in what's working and what's missing.

Faithful Person, Devil's Advocate,

Doubter, Guardian or Rebel

The day they construct strong trust with somebody, they will stick by all of them the path until the end. They are an extremely extraordinary kind of individuals regarding the matter of trust in light of the fact that they have a tendency to trust individuals as much as they doubt individuals in the meantime. These individuals are dependably always searching for something or somebody to have confidence in profoundly – once the individuals they trust in have 'earned their trust', they will be steadfast till death. They have a tendency to respond to apprehension in maybe a couple ways (particularly when their essential obsession of defeatism is showed) either by grasping the trepidation head one (counter-phobic six) or staying away from it no matter what (phobic six).

It's no shock that their heavenly thought is confidence. They generally accept that disregarding their reasons for alarm and vulnerabilities, something great dependably lie around the bend. Their biggest trepidation is detachment and helplessness. They can't live without a solid emotionally supportive network and they can't stand being deserted.

They covet wellbeing most importantly else. They are cynics by nature and will question everything and test everything until it separates however profound inside, they wish to realize that there is no reason to worry. Their greatest allurement is suspiciousness which prompts them doubting thought processes and connections can get to be exceptionally saddling. Their most noteworthy bad habit fear as they are by and large dreadful of numerous things and they relate their lives, their anxieties and their inspirations towards or far from their apprehensions. Notwithstanding, the sort ones are getting it done when they build up the fearlessness to face their apprehensions. Sort sixes with a wing of give are frequently more independent and erudite. They can get to be extremely solid faultfinders. Alternate wings are the sorts that seem all the more obviously anxious. They can likewise erroneously blame others without acknowledging it. They are likewise additionally beguiling and amiable.

Chapter 9: Enneagram And Ancient

Teaching

Chances are you've already heard comments from numerous experts on the Enneagram. As you've already gathered, it is a symbol shrouded in mystical significance and the meaning and its different elements are not always clearly understood. This makes it difficult for some to embrace the idea; the lack of a direct explanation of the whole process often leaves some suspicious and wary, feeling that they may be entering a world of occultism.

For many, the occult is exactly what they think of when looking at the Enneagram symbol. Our minds automatically go there because it so closely resembles the pentagram which is directly connected to modern occultism. This makes many pull back out of fear that they are getting involved in something dangerously mysterious and dark. However, by examining the symbol exclusive of any preconceived notions and clearing your mind from those ideas people tend to automatically associate with it, we begin to see some similarities that we can find in other more acceptable beliefs of our society.

It's a natural part of who we are to want to know more about the origins of anything we get involved in, and while the explanation of the symbol itself can sometimes seem vague and obscure, we have been able to uncover enough to unlock the true meaning of the Enneagram symbol.

However, it is very important to point out that the Enneagram we use today has changed a bit from its original purpose. One of the best ways to decipher it is by starting with the human mind. It is a natural tendency for our human brains to view images and break them down into different categories. Nothing fancy, it's just what the human brain is designed for. Since Gurdjieff is considered to be the father of the modern Enneagram, many will automatically associate the modern Enneagram with his symbol. Gurdjieff's teachings leaned heavily on the metaphysical - a means of organizing natural principles and using them to explain how the universe actually works.

There were three basic principles of Gurdjieff's metaphysical theory, all utilizing the Enneagram symbol. The Law of Seven, Unity, and the Law of Three.

The Law of Seven: this law focused on the constant vibrations we all have around us. It is a little different from the Newtonian physics we have come to understand from modern science. Rather than what we've been taught - an object in motion stays in motion, the Law of Seven sees the world as a series of vibrations. According to this law, each object in motion must pass through seven separate stages before it comes to a stop. This means that the energy is not evenly spent but is instead lost at very specific points before it can receive an additional infusion of energy to continue along its path.

His theory was based on the seven note musical octave with the idea that in nature, once something is in motion, that motion cannot be sustained forever. No matter what it is, it must deviate or change at specific intervals. As you go through a musical scale, for example, as the energy vibrations increase or decrease, the consistent rate naturally changes at certain points. With music, the points have been identified as the mi/fa point, and the si/do point. So, in an octave of do re mi fa so la ti do, the intervals where vibrations change would be between the mi and the fa at one point, and the si and the do at another point.

Of course, there is a lot more to the theory of the Law of Seven that we won't go into here.

According to Gurdjieff, the energy that is spent in vibrations does not uniformly dissipate but instead is lost at very precise points where it can receive an extra impulse to keep it going along its path.

Unity: When you first look at the Enneagram symbol, your eyes will automatically recognize the circle first. This is the universal symbol of unity and infinity. It can also signify the oneness and eternal nature of a Supreme Being. To Gurdjieff, the circle represented two different forms of thinking. First, everything in the universe has a place; everything belongs with no exclusions. And secondly, the symbol was used to encourage a panoramic and more receptive awareness of the whole picture. This is done without judgment or labeling of anything as either good or bad. Anyone who can do this is able therefore to see the world in its true state and not be influenced by prejudices and personal preferences.

The Law of Three or the Triangle: This law represents the union of three fundamental things. First and foremost, the Supreme Being of the universe (God) determines its nature and structure. Secondly, its organizing principle, and finally - the power he has to pull it all together. All three of these elements are key to understanding Gurdjieff's teachings of the Law of Three.

It is clear that Gurdjieff's teachings were extremely complex and detailed but understanding just these basic facts is key to being able to grasp the true purpose of the symbol. As human beings, we have always been in a sort of quandary. On the one hand, we are always in search of our own individuality, but on the other hand, we have a powerful, inbred need to belong to something bigger than ourselves. While the western world leaned more towards seeing the individual to the point where nearly everything became disconnected, the eastern world strived for community and connectivity almost to the complete obliteration of the individual.

When you see the world with more importance placed on connections, the price you pay is a loss of human dignity which is sacrificed for the sake of the whole. On the other hand, when too much importance is placed on the individual, the cost is the infringement on the rights of others. Therefore, the ability to create a balance between the two is essential and having the Spiritual Being holding it all together is key. With a Supreme Being, both unity and diversity can have an equal part in our lives, and we learn to live for both ourselves and for others.

While the ancient history of this symbol may seem vague and elusive, our modern understanding can offer us an even clearer meaning. Today, the symbol is used primarily as a schematic on a number of different personalities.

While the symbol we use today is not exactly the same as the symbol that he used (it has been refined over the decades to be more applicable to the world's society of today), it has many practical applications once you begin to break it down. There are many different ideas as to how to use the symbol. With so many different personalities it is difficult at a glance to know where you actually fit on the personality spectrum. However, you will have some very keen insight into the wisdom of the Enneagram so you can know exactly where you fit in the whole scheme of things.

Today's Enneagram

As we've already pointed out, the structure of the Enneagram is simply a circle with numbers and lines contained within it. Each of these numbers, circles, and lines can be analyzed and viewed from totally different aspects.

At first glance, the idea of a circle with numbered lines doesn't mean very much. At least, not until you begin to learn what each of these markings actually means. In the basic Enneagram symbol, the circle is a symbol of unity. The nine personality types are all equidistant from each other showing that they are all equal to one another. No single personality has more influence or power over any other. In essence, we all start on the same equal footing.

An inner triangle formed by connecting the points at the numbers three, six, and nine. This triangle represents a powerful and dynamic interaction of three different forces.

The Circle: You will see that there are nine different points spaced out around the circumference of the circle. We already understand that the circle is a representation of unity and the nine points are all equidistant from one another. This shows that each personality is equal but still connected to the others.

The Triangle: If you look closely, you will see an inner triangle that connects the three points at three, six, and nine. This represents the dynamic interaction of three very powerful forces. If you were to take two opposites, for example, the connecting force between the two would be some form of middle ground or a blend of each of the polar opposites. Here, three Enneagram Clusters are connected together by the triangle.

Hexad: If you were to look even closer, you would also see an irregular figure that connects all of the other six points. This part of the symbol represents the dynamic change we must all go through. As you will learn later, everyone has their own dominant personality, but it is not in control all the time. We are all constantly switching from one personality to another, each one represented by the Hexad, which connects them all together.

The Numbers: The nine numbers around the circumference represent the nine different personality types. Each type comes with its own seed of motivation that is responsible for triggering certain behaviors. While we all have a mixture of different personality types, we still have a primary or a stronger Enneagram type, which is responsible for our personal views on life, the actions we take, and how we respond to the world around us.

The Arrows: What you may not readily see in some Enneagram symbols are the arrows. However, if you see one with arrow tips at the ends of the lines, you'll notice that they follow a very exact structure that shows just how people shift personalities under varying circumstances. When you are under stress, confident, or achieving a personal level of growth, your behaviors will automatically and instinctively shift from one personality to another within your Cluster. We will move along those connecting paths following the directions of the arrows.

Arrows moving backward represent your stress personality which is your automatic way of separating yourself from your usual behavior and protecting yourself from emotional damage. When some people face severe stress, they could switch to this stress point and remain there before they feel safe enough to return to their dominant personality.

On the other hand, forward pointing arrows travel a path to a more secure place that will permit you to perform safer behaviors. When you are at your security point, you are usually in familiar surroundings with people you can trust. When you are healthy, you might make a move to your Integration Point. This is where you blend together qualities that will create a delicate balance between confidence and structure. If you're looking to grow, it is important that you embrace these Security Points and follow those healthy behaviors applying them in your life.

By now, you've probably already begun to identify with a particular personality type. In fact, you've probably narrowed it down to several. If you're interested in pinpointing exactly which personality type you are, there are several resources you can find online that can help you. Some of them are free but those worth their salt will cost you a little bit of money to take the test. However, the benefits you can gain from this knowledge can be very valuable to you and can help you to improve your life in many different ways.

It is easy to see why so many people are intrigued by the Enneagram and what it can mean for them. It is a tool that gives you the ability to look at your own life and see it for what it really is. It provides the right frame for looking inside and identifying specific patterns that have been influencing your every decision since birth.

With this increased knowledge about yourself, you can feel empowered to venture off into different territories that reach outside of your personal comfort zone. As you do, your life's purpose will become clearer and your course in life, your destiny will unfold before you.

Learning your Enneagram personality is just as much a spiritual journey as it is a psychological one, but if you take it with an open mind, it is possible for you to achieve greater intelligence about the human mind and discover your personal calling. However, it will require you to look deeper below the surface at what's inside for you to do so.

The Iceberg

Humans are highly complex creatures and are made up of many different elements. While we all have the same components, it is the unique combination of those elements that make us individuals. Your personality is made up of a delicate composite of several elements that reflect not just your inner feelings and experiences but also shows up in how you express yourself and interact with those around you.

It has often been described as an iceberg. While the iceberg is massive in size, what you see above the surface of the water are simply those elements that you are consciously aware of. It is the part of our personality that we allow others to see. Beneath the surface, the part of us that either we are not aware of or the part that we will try desperately to hide from those in our lives.

These hidden elements are the very things that drive us to perform certain behaviors. To put it more simply, those hidden parts of our personality can be described as those things that we feel while those things that are visible to our naked eye could be viewed as the elements that inform us and we consciously react to. Together these all encourage our behavior and give us the motivation to do the things we do.

In order for the Enneagram to be most effective and beneficial for us, we must address what is both above and below the line. The combination is what provides us with the insight and the wisdom to make the changes we may feel we need to improve.

Chapter 10: The Three Centers Of

Intelligence

Do you know what it takes for your wife/husband, lover, or significant other to feel absolutely and completely loved? What are his or her chief concerns in life? How do they spend their time when they are alone with their mind?

Our research indicates that people have the experience of feeling love in primarily three specific ways. Some people need to be touched in specific ways to know that they are being loved. These people operate primarily out of their bodies, are physically or kinesthetically oriented, and tend to have issues around anger. Some people have to be shown that they are loved by bringing them flowers and other presents, taking them places, and doing things for them. These people operate primarily out of their emotions, are feeling oriented, and have issues with image and relationships. The third group of people needs to be told that they are loved in specific ways, depending upon the individual. These people operate out of their minds, are mentally based, and have issues around fear.

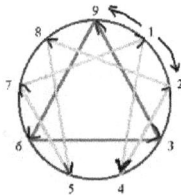

Each of these love strategies, when combined with various intensities and mental, emotional, physical concerns give rise to the nine personality types. The set of types is a system that describes nine basic personality types and their mental and emotional preoccupations and concerns. Our goal is not to make a complete presentation of the personality, as this has already been excellently explored by others. Rather, I wish to present a small précis of each type in order for us to understand how to improve our relationships with our wives, girl/boyfriends, and significant others.

Examine the diagram on the left. The first thing to notice is the central triangle connecting points 3, 6, and 9 in red. These points represent the "core" personalities from which the surrounding points, otherwise known as "wings," derive their primary concerns, as discussed above. The wings are connected by the lines 1-4-2-8-5-7-1 as show in green. The lines represent movement from one point to another in response to changing conditions in life. Movement along the direction of the arrows is usually in response to stress. Thus, under stress, a point 1 will move to point 4, etc. Movement in the opposite direction usually indicates a secure life situation. For example, a point 6 will go into point 9 when feeling secure.

Within each type, there are central emotional and mental issues that preoccupy a person of a given type and give rise to the love strategies discussed previously. These preoccupations cause attention to be fixated or locked into specific patterns of behavior which produce difficulties for the self and others. According to the types, the mental preoccupations for each type are traditionally called the fixations, which are illustrated in Diagram 2, and the emotional preoccupations are called the passions, which are shown in Diagram 3. Correspondingly, there are high functioning mental and emotional aspects of each type, which are called the holy ideas and virtues, respectively. These characteristics have been presented in diagrams, the Holy Ideas, and the Virtues (above).

The Three Centers

The traditional exposition of the types begins with an explanation of the three centers from which man operates, and in general, there are three types of men and women. The three centers are the head center, the heart center and the belly center.

All three centers are active in each person, and are necessary for survival. However, the mentally-based man or woman operates primarily out of the head center, the emotionally-based man or woman operates primarily out of the heart center, and the belly-based man or woman operates out of the belly center. To complete the picture outlined above, that any love strategy can be adopted by any personality type, but the head-based person tends to adopt a love strategy which requires them to hear that they are loved. Similarly, the heart-based person tends to adopt a "show me" strategy, and belly-based people like to be touched in specific ways.

You have all known intelligent thinkers who seem to be lost in their heads, figuring out how their world works, creating scientific wonders, or the typical "nerdy" computer programmer. In this category, we find the compulsive "planners", who like to experience everything in life but are impossible to pin down. Trying to get one of these types out on a hike or off on a ski weekend is like pulling teeth! However, some of us do enjoy the outdoors and getting "out of our heads" from time to time.

Similarly, you have noticed hysterical emotional types who remind us of how strong feelings can become. These can be demonstrated in different types of people such as the creative artist who can move us with the stroke of a brush or the sound of their voice, and the sensitive listener who cares about not only our problems but everyone else's. These people operate from their emotions, but still have to retreat into their minds to balance their checkbooks, follow recipes, or discuss the merits of the latest political campaigns.

Finally, we watch the belly-based athletes perform feats of strength and endurance on Monday Night Football or during the World Series. These men and women could also be excellent performers, and their focus of attention is in their gut. We have also seen abusive bullies (type eight) portrayed in countless movies and maddening perfectionists standing up for what they think is correct.

The nine types reflect the tendencies of these three basic types - the mental types, emotional types, and physical types.

The Mental Types

Points of the Head Center

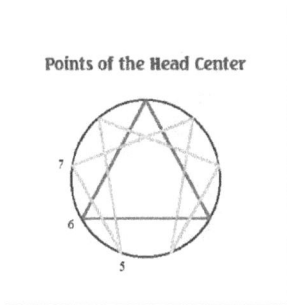

The core emotional issue of the mental types is fear. The fear that we are referring to is a fear of real or imagined danger that manifest in the scanning of the environment for threatening situations. It is this primary concern with fear that drives the love strategy that these types adopt. They need constant reassurance that everything is okey and that they will be loved in spite of their actions. It is beneficial for head-based people to even request confirmation of where they stand with their loved ones, rather than assuming the worst case scenario and doubting the love.

Type 6

Type six represents the point which is most out of touch with their fear. There is the phobic six, who avoids fearful situations by totally evading them, and the counter-phobic six who attacks fearful situations with a dauntless semblance of courage. The phobic sixes would do anything to move away from a fearful situation. They vigilantly scan the surroundings to attempt to discover and disarm any imminent peril. They try to do whatever they can in order to feel safe.

On the other hand, the counter-phobic sixes enjoy "safe and easy" things like sky diving, race care driving, mountain climbing and other sports which directly confront danger. In actuality, they don't feel much bothered by fear in these circumstances. It seems to drive their adrenaline up to exciting levels. However hard they try to deny it, the basis for their action is fear. This is not to say that all race car drivers are sixes, but you will find that some of them are.

Type 5

Type five was said to be the type that is most withdrawn from fear. They like to retreat into a mental world and to review their feelings in the privacy of their own homes. They tend to be highly intellectual and withdrawn into themselves.

Type 7

Type seven represents the point which is most externalized with respect to fear. People of this type have adopted the strategy of diffusing fear into pleasant options. They tend to be charming, lovable people for whom nothing is apparently wrong.

All of the fear types need constant reassurance that they are loved and also to find out what the parameters are in any relationship. One of their basic strategies in life should be to ascertain where they stand in a relationship, be it romantic or business.

The Emotional Types

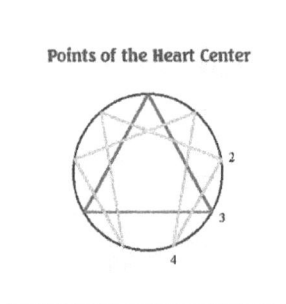

Points of the Heart Center

The core emotional issue for the feeling types is an overriding concern for image. They have to deal with questions about how they are feeling. Because of their overwhelming concern for image, the heart-based types appreciate the little things that you can give them (diamonds, rubies, pearls, Lexus, etc.), as well as the romantic places you can take them for quick get-a-way weekends or nights out on the town. By the way, they don't mind pretty dresses, works of art, and home-

106

cooked meals that they don't have to prepare!

Type 3

Type three represents the type which is most out of touch with their feelings. In this type of person, the feelings are suspended for the sake of performance, making a good impression, and getting the job done. They are concerned with efficiency and meeting deadlines. Many "work-alcoholic" people are threes.

Type 4

Type four was said to represent the internalized version of feelings. They tend to be highly emotional people with artistic temperaments and a love for aesthetics. They like intensity in all of its forms.

Type 2

Type two was said to be the most externally oriented about their feelings. They have the ability to alter themselves to meet the needs of the people in their environment and get a lot out of giving to others. During the course of this almost excessive giving, they suppress their own needs.

Emotional types usually want to be shown that they are loved

The Body Types

Points of the Belly Center

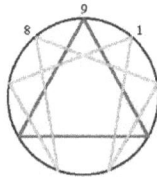

The core emotional issue for the physical types is anger. As such, anger originates in the body and finds expression in various ways. The gut-based people like to be touched in special places that turn them on to the feelings they have inside their bodies. A special caress or a gentle touch can go further to demonstrate your love for them than almost anything else.

Type 9

Type nine is said to be the most out of touch with anger. Because of this, nines are passive-aggressive and want to do anything they can to avoid the direct expression of their anger. While they are extremely amiable, they tend to be terribly self-forgetting and merge with others' points of views.

Type 1

Type one represents the internalized version of anger. Their anger is addressed at a righteous cause or maintaining a correct posture about important elements in their lives. The ones tend to be perfectionistic about everything they feel, think and do in life.

Type 8

Type eight represents the type which is most expressive about their anger. Here we have the outspoken leader or boss who can present their anger at a moment's notice. They have no qualms about letting out their anger, even if it may be inappropriate behavior.

Love Strategies

Now what happens if your love strategy is different from your partners? Suppose you are the type who wants to be shown that you are loved, but your partner is one of the other types. Here you go marching off to the ends of the world to buy her fancy things and all she wants is to be told how much you love her or to be touched in those specific ways that let her know that you really care. What do you do in this situation? How do you find out what type your partner is?

Obviously, with understanding, comes love and compassion. We all have our faults and strong points. Understanding begins with ourselves and then moves on to the other people in our lives: our significant other, parents, children, friends, and acquaintances.

About this book

This book is a product of forty years of work with the enneagram system of personality types and their potentials. It was originally presented in a different form to members of various groups I participated in over the years. Some of the material first appeared on the web as early as 1996. Used in conjunction with exercises to awaken your potential, known affectionately as it can lead you on your path to well-being.

Awaken Your Potential!

The series of books with accompanying audio instructions that comprise the Awaken Your Potential series consist of attention practices also known as mindfulness practices designed to increase your awareness of your inner processes and elevate your sense of self-empowerment and self-worth. You will learn to pay attention to what is going on in your heart, mind and body in the present moment on purpose without judging the experience. The practices are designed to increase your awareness of your body, feelings and emotions and thoughts. From these exercises, you will achieve a sense of your inner heart-mind, which is your own true nature. Consequently, your sense of generosity and compassion will increase greatly and you will feel more fulfilled.

Some of the titles in this series are:

☐ Awaken Your Breath

☐ **Awaken Your Body**

☐ Awaken Your Feelings

☐ Awaken Your Thoughts

☐ Awaken Your Healing Potential

☐ Awaken Your Parenting Ability

☐ Awaken Your Relaxation Response

☐ Awaken Your Creativity

☐ Awaken Your Compassionate Caring

☐ Awaken to Sitting Quietly

☐ Awaken Your Desire to Eat Healthy Foods

☐ Awaken Your Fitness

☐ Awaken to Walking Mindfully

☐ Awaken in Daily Life

☐ Awaken Your Contemplative Practice

☐ Awaken to Planning and Setting Goals

☐ Awaken Your Insight

The first book in this series, Awaken Your Potential – Awaken Your Breath should be available by the time you read this.

Furthering Your Potential

The best way to learn about your type and your potential is to observe a panel of people who know their type. The exemplars are interviewed by a trained professional who knows what questions to ask to bring out the personality types and the potentials of the participants. Since there are nine personality types, it would be optimal to observe nine different panels over a period of nine evenings in a classroom setting. Through the questions and responses, you can get a feeling for your type if you feel a resonance with what the exemplars are saying.

Finally, reading books about personality types can provide some insight, but the process can take considerably longer than the previous options. There are many books and web sites about this topic, and you have a great start from the know your type test, the yourtype.org web site, and this book.

Adopting the attention practices by subscribing to the book series of the previous section is virtually guaranteed to optimize your potential. Taking time to practice can open your heart, mind and body to experience the wonders of life every day. Even short moments of awareness will now begin to crop up in your daily activities at work or at play.

Origin of the Diagram

The structure of the diagram, with the nine points and the lines connecting them, was first introduced into the West by George Gurdjieff, a mystic who was born in the area between Greece and the Caspian Sea in the late 1860s or early 1870s and flourished in Europe in the early 20th century. He called the diagram the enneagram, which simply means a nine sided diagram. The concept of identifying personality type was introduced by Oscar Ichazo and developed by Dr. Claudio Naranjo.

Chapter 11: The Enneagram Personality

Type 4 - The Artist

Also called the Individualist or the Romantic, the Artist is driven by the need to be unique. This person needs to feel different and special and is constantly on an identity search. This person is trying to build their identity so that they appear different to others and as a result they are often self-conscious. They often see their differences from others as being a gift or a curse because it so sharply sets them apart from others. They see this difference as a gift when it allows them to not fall into a category of commonality with others. They see it as a curse when they feel like it sets them apart from happiness, serenity, and joy.

What Makes the Artist a Great Personality

THE ARTIST IS HIGHLY EXPRESSIVE. Because these types of people seek the uniqueness in themselves and in life, they are often highly expressive and turn to creative careers like painting, writing, and other forms of art.

THE ARTIST IS SELF-AWARE. The basic desire of the Artist is to find themselves and their significance in this world. They want to create a unique identity for themselves and therefore, strive to do just that. As a result, these personality types often surround themselves with beauty to create moods and feelings that express individuality and express their unique nature. Type 4s also acknowledge and accept their own feelings and do not try to whitewash them. They are not afraid to see their own perceived flaws either.

THE ARTIST IS INDIVIDUALISTIC. Because of the brutally honest introspection, Artists tend to be true to themselves and develop a high sense of individuality. Type 4s are sensitive souls and often concerned with self-expression and self-revelation. They often outwardly express this with idiosyncrasies in the way that they dress and their overall demeanor.

The Deadly Sins of the Artist

THE ARTIST IS MISUNDERSTOOD. This person is searching for depth in themselves and their relationships and cannot stand shallow interactions and experiences. Because of the differences that they have, Artists often feel superior to others even though they have a feeling of longing and envy because deeply they want to be understood and appreciated by others. This contradiction means that they are misunderstood and underappreciated by others. This also encourages fears of being flawed or defective since they do not fit into the typical mold. This means that Artists are typically moody and withdrawn from others. Others often perceive them as being temperamental. This can be because they are often in their own internal world where they constantly analyze their feelings. Type 4s often have trouble staying in the moment and can lose themselves in nostalgia.

THE ARTIST OFTEN SUFFERS FROM MENTAL ILLNESS. Because of their overall melancholy disposition, type 4s tend to lapse into depression very easily and can become mentally and emotionally unbalanced because of this self-absorption.

THE ARTIST IS OFTEN SELF-INDULGENT. They give in to self-indulgence very easily and justify this as a way of compensating for the lack of pleasure in their lives generally. Type 4s are prone to thinking of fantasies to alleviate the problems rather than looking for practical solutions to solve the unhappy.

THE ARTIST IS OFTEN EMOTIONALLY DISCONNECTED. Because of the tendency to be stuck in their own head, type 4s often miss out on the joy of participating in a given situation or a given moment. They often feel a deep sense of disappointment when life does not live up to what happens in their heads. They are often easily swept away by their own emotions and feel more comfortable in the darker emotional spectrum rather than the happy light side of things.

How Artists Relate to Other Personality Types

Artists vs. Type 1s

Please see Chapter 2: How Reformers Relate to Other Personality Types: Reformers vs. Type 4s.

Artists vs. Type 2s

Please see Chapter 3: How Helpers Relate to Other Personality Types: Helpers vs. Type 4s.

Artists vs. Type 3s

Please see Chapter 4: How Performers Relate to Other Personality Types: Performers vs. Type 4s.

Artists vs. Type 5s

Both of these personality types are extremely private and, while they may have different interests, they can both appreciate and respect each other's intensity and commitment to their values and feelings. Generally, these two personality types find each other stimulating and are respectful of each other's idiosyncrasies. They inspire each other to be more creative. Conflict may arise because the Artist is more emotional and tends to need deeper contact and intimacy than type 5s. Type 5s tend to push away from emotional attachment because they are thinking types and prefer space in their relationships.

Artists vs. Type 6s

These two personality types are naturally attracted to each other because they are both highly emotional and feel insecure around other people. They are both highly intuitive and as such they are often mistaken for each other. When they both work on the emotional issues, a union between these two personality types is a recipe for steadfast endurance and practicality. Issues may arise between them for the same reason that they are attracted to each other - the deeply emotional nature. Both are very emotionally volatile and can easily feel overwhelmed. They tend to test each other's loyalty and quickly feel a sense of abandonment. Both personality types tend to create self-fulfilling prophecies in their fears and reactions to their relationships.

Artists vs. Type 7s

When these two personality types form a relationship, it is a matter of opposites attracting. Type 4s are emotional, self-doubting, introverted, and quiet while type 7s are more outgoing, confident, extroverted, and optimistic. Type 7s can help the Artist overcome issues of shyness, a reluctance to try new experiences, and to get out of their feelings while the Artist can help the Enthusiast stay focused on the things that they truly want. These two personality types think and react differently but these differences can help them find pleasure in each other. Again, issues may arise because of their differences because they both tend to be impulsive and get easily frustrated with others when they feel that they have been disappointed.

Artists vs. Type 8s

While the Artist is emotionally dominant and type 8 is socially dominant, these two can bring fire and passion into a relationship because they are both highly intuitive, self-aware, and knowledgeable about how they feel. They are both intense personality types and can match each other. Because both types are so reactive, their relationship can be volatile in a negative way with periods of rage, vengeance, and depression. They are prone to having arguments and fights rather than approaching conflict with level heads.

Artists vs. Type 9s

Both of these personality types are withdrawn, private, and emotionally sensitive. They both seek a deep connection with another person and as such can be a supportive pair to each other. Both of these personality types are naturally sensual and love the comfort of being able to express themselves so intimately with someone else. Problems may arise when these two personality types react differently to stressful stimuli. Type 4s can become emotionally volatile while type 9s become withdrawn. These different approaches can make it very difficult to solve conflict in a relationship leading to its deterioration.

How the Artist Can Improve His or Her Life

This person needs to become more grounded in the present moment and to become more in touch with their bodies and less with their emotions. They need to develop a holistic identity and learn to control their emotions rather than being swept away by them. Practicing root and heart chakra meditation helps keep them grounded in reality and become more compassionate towards themselves and others. In addition, they may also practice navel chakra meditation to increase their self-esteem and assertive qualities. Navel chakra meditation starts by putting your hands before your stomach, just below your solar plexus. All fingers need to be joined at the tips. Cross the thumbs and keep your fingers straight. While chanting, concentrate on the navel chakra located on the spine just above the level of the navel.

Acupressure is also helpful. In addition to stimulating the points SP-6 and LIV-3, LI 4 can be stimulated to let go of grief while the stimulation of LU-1 allows for connecting with one's inner worth. L1-4 is found on the top side of the hand between the thumb and index finger where they are connected by the web of Flesh. LU-1 is located on the chest just underneath the shoulder.

Other practical solutions that the Artist can practice to improve his or her life include:

●Not placing so much emphasis on how they are feeling.

●Realizing that their emotions in that moment are limited only to that moment and may not be more important than that.

●Avoiding lengthy conversations with their imaginations, especially if those conversations are excessively negative or resentful.

●Not placing things on the back burner until they are in the right mood.

●Committing to being productive and working consistently in the "real world."

●Pursuing activities that develop their self-esteem and self-confidence.

●Committing to regular sleeping hours and exercise to improve their positivity and outlook on life.

●Practicing self-discipline and avoiding activities that have a negative impact on their lives such as excessive sexual experiences, drugs, alcohol, and sleep.

Chapter 12: The Investigator Subtypes

The three subtypes associated with the investigator are castle, confidant, and totem. You can learn more about these subtypes and what they mean below.

Self-preservation: Castle

The investigator has a tendency to be very protective over their privacy and their personal space. They are known for having very clear boundaries and limits and tend to enjoy living their life in a solitary manner. The investigator may only have very few close friends, and no one else can be noteworthy in their life. This allows them to keep themselves preserved and ensures that the individuals they are interacting with will definitely adhere to their strict personal boundaries.

Investigators often find themselves preferring to observe others socializing or living their lives versus actually doing it themselves. They are typically the truest form of introvert to exist. They do not typically prefer to reveal themselves to other people, as they find it difficult to do so. They like to keep their guard up to refrain from losing their privacy or the security they experience by staying solitary and with strict boundaries.

One-on-One: Confidant

Due to the solitary and quiet nature of the investigator, they tend to be very passionate about and loyal to the few close people that they have in their lives. They will typically find themselves experiencing a strong chemistry with those close in their lives and find enjoyment in the level of intensity that this brings to their relationship. This allows them to feel very trustworthy and open to their close ones.

The investigator will risk the feeling of depending on the other people they are close with as a way to make them feel vibrant and alive in their lives. This can result in them periodically "testing" the loyalty of those in their lives to see if the same intensity is returned. They may even become possessive and resist sharing these people with anyone else.

Social: Totem

Investigators are known to look for the deeper or hidden meaning in virtually every situation. They ask big questions and love to pursue wisdom and seek greater levels of knowledge. They are typically highly passionate about connecting with groups or specific experts who are brilliant in the topics that the investigator is most passionate about. Although they love sharing in these group settings, they may resist sharing any of their space, time, or resources too much. Instead, they prefer to absorb, observe, and learn from others while quietly accumulating their own knowledge.

They tend to be quite disconnected from everyday emotions and issues that the average person faces. They may even find themselves disconnecting from people around them altogether, preferring to preserve their energy to learn more.

Chapter 13: Type One – The Reformer

Enneagram Type 1, the Reformer: Best and Worst Careers

It is safe to say that you are pondering about what kinds of professions are best for you, in view of your Enneagram test results? In case you're a Type 1, these are the best Enneagram type 1 professions (and the most exceedingly terrible!).

What is an Enneagram character type?

First of all, Enneagram tests are like the great Myers-Briggs Type Indicator (MBTI) test. Basically, an Enneagram encourages you locate the particular qualities that make up your character type.

As indicated by the Enneagram Institute, there are nine Enneagram types and "it is entirely expected to locate a tad bit of yourself in each of the nine of the sorts, albeit one of them should stand apart as being nearest to yourself." The one that stands apart is "your essential character type."

The nine Enneagram types incorporate the accompanying:

The Reformer — the discerning and optimistic sort

The Helper — the minding and relational sort

The Achiever (some of the time alluded to as the Motivator) — the achievement arranged and down to earth type

The Individualist (some of the time alluded to as the Artist) — the touchy and pulled back type

The Investigator (here and there alluded to as the Thinker) — the extraordinary and cerebral sort

The Loyalist (in some cases alluded to as the Skeptic) — the submitted and security-situated sort

The Enthusiast (now and then alluded to as the Generalist) — the outgoing and unconstrained sort

The Challenger (now and then alluded to as the Leader) — the incredible and commanding sort

The Peacemaker — the nice and self-destroying type

So, you can likewise have a wing type. "Typically, one has attributes of one of the sorts that falsehood contiguous one's own that are increasingly noticeable — this is known as the wing," as indicated by Electric Energies. "So, somebody who is a sort 5, may have a 4 wing or a 6 wing. This might be condensed to '5w4' and '5w6.' If one doesn't have a predominant wing, it is said that the wings are adjusted."

1 - THE REFORMER

Enneagram Type One

The Rational, Idealistic Type:

Principled, Purposeful, Self-Controlled, and Perfectionistic

Type One in a nutshell

Ones are principled and moral, with a solid feeling of good and bad. They are educators, crusaders, and supporters for change: continually endeavoring to improve things, yet scared of committing an error. Efficient, deliberate, and particular, they attempt to keep up elevated expectations, yet can slip into being basic and perfectionistic. They normally have issues with hatred and fretfulness. At their best: savvy, observing, sensible, and honorable. Can be ethically chivalrous.

Essential Fear: Of being degenerate/abhorrent, deficient

Essential Desire: To be great, to have respectability, to be adjusted

Enneagram One with a Nine-Wing: "The Idealist"

Enneagram One with a Two-Wing: "The Advocate"

Key Motivations: Want to be right, to endeavor higher and improve everything, to be reliable with their standards, to legitimize themselves, to be past analysis so as not to be censured by anybody.

The Meaning of the Arrows (in a word)

While moving in their Direction of Disintegration (stress), systematic Ones all of a sudden become testy and silly at Four.

Nonetheless, while moving in their Direction of Integration (development), irate, basic Ones become increasingly unconstrained and upbeat, as sound Sevens. Become familiar with the bolts.

Models: Confucius, Plato, Salahuddin Ayyubi, Joan of Arc, Sir Thomas More, Mahatma Gandhi, Pope John Paul II, Nelson Mandela, Margaret Thatcher, Prince Charles, Kate Middleton, Duchess of Cambridge, Jimmy Carter, Michelle Obama, Al Gore, Hilary Clinton, Rudy Giuliani, Elliot Spitzer, Justice Sandra Day O'Connor, Osama receptacle Laden, George Bernard Shaw, Thoreau, Dr. Jack Kevorkian, Anita Roddick (The Body Shop), Martha Stewart, Chef Thomas Keller, Michio Kushi (macrobiotics), George Harrison, Joan Baez, Celine Dion, Ralph Nader, Noam Chomsky, Bill Moyers, George F. Will, William F. Buckley, Keith Olbermann, Jerry Seinfeld, Bill Maher, Tina Fey, Katherine Hepburn, Maggie Smith, Emma Thompson, Julie Andrews, Vanessa Redgrave, Jane Fonda, Meryl Streep, Harrison Ford, Helen Hunt, Captain "Sully"

Sullenberger, "Mary Poppins," "Mr. Spock," SNL's "The Church Lady"

Type One Overview

We have named character type One The Reformer since Ones have a "feeling of strategic" drives them to need to improve the world in different manners, utilizing whatever level of impact they have. They endeavor to beat misfortune—especially moral affliction—with the goal that the human soul can radiate through and have any kind of effect. They make progress toward "higher qualities," even at the expense of extraordinarilyy giving up one's own priorities.

History is brimming with Ones who have left agreeable lives to accomplish something phenomenal in light of the fact that they felt that something higher was calling them. During the Second World War, Raoul Wallenburg left an agreeable white-collar class life to work for the insurance of thousands of European Jews from attacking Nazis. In India, Gandhi abandoned his better half and family and life as an effective legal advisor to turn into a nomad backer of Indian autonomy and peaceful social changes. Joan of Arc left her town in France to reestablish the position of authority to the Dauphin and to oust the English from the nation. The optimism of every one of these Ones has roused millions.

Ones are individuals of pragmatic activity—they wish to be valuable in the best feeling of the word. In some capacity of awareness, they feel that they "have a crucial" satisfy throughout everyday life, if just to attempt their best to lessen the turmoil they find in their condition.

Albeit Ones have a solid feeling of direction, they likewise normally feel that they need to legitimize their activities to themselves, and frequently to others too. This direction makes Ones invest a ton of energy considering the results of their activities, just as about how to prevent from acting in opposition to their feelings. Along these lines, Ones regularly convince themselves that they are "head" types, realists who continue just on rationale and target truth. However, the genuine picture is to some degree unique: Ones are really activists who are looking for a worthy basis for what they believe they should do. They are individuals of impulse and energy who use feelings and decisions to control and direct themselves and their activities.

What is the Enneagram type 1 character?

Type 1, the Reformer, is "the normal, optimistic sort" that is "principled, deliberate, self-controlled and perfectionistic," as indicated by the Enneagram Institute. "Ones are upright and moral, with a solid feeling of good and bad. They are instructors, crusaders and backers for change: continually endeavoring to improve things, yet terrified of committing an error. Efficient, deliberate and fussy, they attempt to keep up exclusive expectations yet can slip into being basic and perfectionistic. They ordinarily have issues with disdain and restlessness."

This is what you should think about an Enneagram type 1 character more or less:

Their essential apprehensions incorporate being degenerate or shrewd and imperfect.

Their essential wants incorporate being great, having respectability and being adjusted.

Their key inspirations are to be correct and endeavor higher to improve all parts of their lives. In like manner, they work to be predictable with their beliefs and to legitimize those standards (and themselves).

Some great instances of type 1 characters incorporate Confucius, Plato, Joan of Arc, Gandhi, Pope John Paul II, Nelson Mandela, Kate Middleton, Michelle Obama, Al Gore, Hilary Clinton, Tina Fey, Katherine Hepburn, Meryl Streep, Harrison Ford and that's just the beginning.

Type 1 characters are named reformers since, "ones have a 'feeling of crucial' drives them to need to improve the world in different manners, utilizing whatever level of impact they have. They endeavor to defeat difficulty — especially moral affliction — with the goal that the human soul can radiate through and have any kind of effect," as indicated by the Enneagram Institute. "They seek out 'higher qualities,' even at the expense of incredibly giving up of one's own priorities."

What are the attributes of a kind 1?

Here are a few qualities of a kind 1 character:

1. Normal

Type 1 characters are judicious in their activities who will in general continue just on rationale and target truth. They're sensible on account of their capacity to legitimize, which is surely an alluring quality.

2. Principled

Type 1-character types are additionally inconceivably principled individuals who will in general need to be reasonable, objective and moral to the exclusion of everything else. They adhere to reality and worth equity, as they have a solid awareness of other's expectations and trustworthiness.

3. Intentional

Type 1 characters invest a great deal of energy considering their activities and the effect of those activities. Thus, they will in general act with reason. They have a lot more grounded feeling of direction than other character types, and they likewise will in general feel that they need to legitimize their activities to themselves and frequently to others in light of that reason.

What are the best professions for type 1 characters?

There are huge amounts of occupations in which the reformer type would exceed expectations. In any case, here are seven to kick you off.

1. Educators

Type 1 characters are "efficient, systematic and meticulous," as indicated by the Enneagram Institute. They intend to keep up exclusive requirements, and maintain those principles in schools as teachers. Since they're likewise deliberate, being experts in their fields enables them to help show undergrad and graduate understudies as educators, with aims to enable their understudies to develop into professions like their own.

2. Judges

Type 1 characters have confidence in reality, keep up objectivity and have a great deal of uprightness. Thus, they make extraordinary judges. "Very principled, consistently need to be reasonable, objective and moral: truth and equity essential qualities. Awareness of other's expectations, individual respectability and of having a higher reason regularly make them educators and observers to reality," as per the Enneagram Institute.

3. Cops

Once more, since type 1-character types care such a great amount about maintaining measures, they make committed cops who maintain the law.

4. Ecological Specialists

Type 1 characters are the reformist kinds who need to make change and do well in employments that fill a need — particularly a reason about which they're enthusiastic. As condition masters, they can help have an effect on the world.

5. Dissident

Type 1 characters are enthusiastic and intentional. They have a serious feeling of good and bad and individual convictions, and they're willing to battle for what's privilege and what they wholeheartedly put stock in.

6. Social Workers

Type 1-character types make exceptional social specialists since they long for having an effect on others' lives. They will in general be reasonable and know the best following stages, and they can help other people to make those strides and turn their lives around.

7. Criminologists

Type 1 characters are fixated on reality. What's more, as analysts, they can invest their energy burrowing for it.

Chapter 14: Mean Business

Generally, the Enneagram is used by a facilitator. This could be a couples'

counselor, therapist, workplace manager, research student, et cetera. The

Enneagram is meant to be used as a process; a means to an end. Whoever is

facilitating will need to have advanced knowledge of the Enneagram and how it

works. Additionally, they will need to be open and challenge answers given by

participants to encourage them to open up about their personalities.

This process works best when it is led by someone who is there as a service to the

individuals attending the group. If you apply the Enneagram as a process, it gives

the user a tool to improve communication, resolve conflicts and offer a level of trust

between the group. It also works best as a coaching tool rather than a rulebook.

Managers or coaches can enhance retention through learning how each person is

motivated by what tasks, cultures, and values. The facilitator can then discover how

to best reward individuals to produce the best response. If we can appreciate our

differences, we can expand the communication between personnel and the

organization and improving the odds of retaining workforces and enhancing

results. We can get a generalized idea of how to use the Process Enneagram to

apply in business using research information from several different sources over

the last 50 years.

Since the beginning of the industrial revolution, it was thought that employees will

be driven to perform based on how they view their efforts are compensated. For example, if Sally is happy with her current compensation, she will continue to

produce consistently. However, if she is unhappy she may produce more or less. If

she values money, she may performer better. If her value is on something other

than money, she may perform less.

More modern theories add goal-setting as a necessity for encouraging personnel

and view desires and ethics as the determining factor of goals. Related findings

highlight specific groups: CAREER DEVELOPMENT (including mentorship, training and

development, and advancement), MEANINGFUL WORK that speaks to an individual's

CAREER GOALS, organizational culture and reputation, acknowledgment, leadership

support, positive employment processes, AND competitive, skills-based

 COMPENSATION AND BENEFITS. Focusing on these groups are thought to assist organizations in hiring great employees and keeping them.

Chapter 15: Your Typing Tunnel

Verifying Your Number Type

Here is more information to verify your character type. Do this next section of the book to see how your typical behaviours and attitudes, beliefs and values impact on the choice you have made and further confirm your choice of type. Or, let's see how maybe you wish to try another number on for size until you find your true fit. The important thing here is that YOUR decision will equal YOUR numbered personality type.

IMPORTANT: There are Ten Sections within the Tunnel. At the end of each section make a note of your preferred choice, as there is an answer page in the Chapter 'YOUR DECISION = YOUR NUMBER!' which will reveal your number type based on your preferences. Have fun!

1.Find Your Triad

The Enneagram is split into three distant triads and each one has its own unique qualities.

Now, we are all invested in all three triads, in that we all have a bit of genuine gut instinct from time to time and we all have a heart and can be very feeling and of course, we all use our head! However, there is one that is MORE influential than the others.

I shall describe them below and then you must choose the one triad you are most drawn to.

The Gut

If I am in this triad I shoot first and ask questions later!

I can have flashes of intense energy and often experience 'knee jerk' reactions to life.

People have sometimes said to me 'Why don't you just THINK before you do things?' Or, 'SEE! I told you to be more careful!' Or, 'Can't you just sit down for a moment!' Or, 'I thought you were all enthusiastic yesterday - and now you really don't seem bothered at all, what happened?'

The body is really important me, which is either utilised greatly with lots of emphasis on how things taste and smell and the pleasure the body can give, or conversely (because of the sensations of the body that this triad is more sensitive to than other triad types) they seek to anaesthetise themselves by using food or alcohol to deaden oneself to that sensitivity, or to cope with having to 'ignore' the body's messages if having to work long hours for example.

I usually take practical action, even if others disagree, because I think I am doing the right thing, or that I HAVE to do SOMETHING here even if it is NOT the right thing, or distract myself from what is going on. I sometimes just go off and DO things and maybe try to surprise other people spontaneously and I think they will be delighted and sometimes they are more shocked than pleased! I can change

150

my mind in an instant and sometimes regret it.

I want to have impact on the world and experience true rage, if I allow myself to accept that, which is often modified into resentment or an enforced 'it doesn't really matter' attitude to save me from fully admitting just how annoying something is!

As I focus on the world and folks around me, I can be somewhat 'self forgetting'.

DECISION TIME!

Does this sound like you? If yes, make a note of 'The Gut', if not, disregard and move to next section.

The Head

If I am in this triad I am very aware of what could possibly happen that I think and plan to safeguard against bad things happening and plot my way to more pleasurable status.

I am quite a relational person and am full of ideas.

I think THEN act and I figure things out. The mental realm is important to me, finding our information (whether to find more pleasure or safeguard against danger or to further my knowledge bank). I need to have enough, or more than enough. There is fear, pain and doubt in the world and thinking it through can somewhat compensate for that.

People sometimes say to me, 'So have you decided what you are going to do yet?' Or, 'Surely to goodness you know that by now, let's go!' Or, 'We will figure it out when we get there'. Or, 'Oh, right, another one of your bright ideas, eh?'

DECISION TIME!

Does this sound like you? If yes, make a note 'The Head', if not, disregard and move to next section.

The Heart

If I am in this triad I am quite aware of how I am feeling most of the time and take steps to address those feelings.

I am alert to how others feel about me too and want to be acknowledged and thought of as significant in life.

I don't like being made a fool of and insults and criticisms hit me hard. I experience shame quite easily so I guard against it by being someone that other people like, respect and admire.

It is quite easy for me to be what is required at the time, the focused and diligent worker, the avid helper or by being very different to the norm, being the best at my endeavor. This is important to me.

In big decisions, I need to feel it is the right thing for me, though my head tells me one thing, if it doesn't FEEL right then it really bothers me.

DECISION TIME!

Does this sound like you? If yes, make a note 'The Heart'.

Chapter 16: Type Six: The Cautious Caregiver

In This Chapter:

Fight or flight

Fears both real and imagined Be prepared!

Nothing is certain - can you handle it? I have a question!

Identifying the six in others and Yourself

Of all the types, Sixes least like to be typed, a real cue to typing a Six. Fear is a core feature, often surfacing in worst- case thinking. Insecurity has them asking questions—many, many questions. Even when they are silent, the inner questions are endless. Being predisposed to doubt, they often feel more secure with problems than when things are going well. Danger is approaching? Sixes leap into the breach, being familiar with problems and liking to be prepared. Problems can even make a Six feel more secure. If things get too stable, you may notice Sixes intentionally creating new problems.

Nonverbal cues

Sixes tend to challenge assumptions, can interrupt with questions, have a nervous energy, look for definition from others, and have issues with authority. Sixes can be black and white and be judgmental, like Ones. Their judgments are not as much out of morality, like Ones, but are out of concern for the safest outcomes. When secure, Sixes can be great listeners. When not, they challenge and test everything you say. They can have strong opinions, mostly to ensure security.

Some of Sixes nonverbal cues include: Being definite and then doubting Listening intently for problems

Noticing EXIT signs, or the need for extra safety equipment

Scanning with eyes back and forth to check everything out, then forward to check and focus, then back to think and analyze

A quizzical, concerned, or doubtful facial expression Cornering others to question what is true or real

verbal cues

Asking questions to either achieve certainty or clarify the uncertain

A questioning, argumentative, or doubting tone

Labeling, needing to define things without leaving space for complexity

Vacillating by changing their mind Asking about your credentials

sixes in caregiving

Cautious Sixes scan for danger. These changeable times have so many unknowns that it is easy to imagine danger. Because it is so changeable, it is a job to keep it nailed down! Not always trusting in relationships to be a support, you check for deeper motivations to determine what is real, always questioning. Once a relationship has been tested, you are loyal and expect the same from others.

All caregivers are fearful and vigilant at times, but for Sixes that is their preset state. As a Six, you are wired to prepare for worst-case possibilities which, during caregiving, can be an invaluable skill at certain times. But can you tell the difference between real dangers, and concerns that are generated in the mind? Do you live too much in a state of fear? If this feels like you then you are likely a Six.

At the best of times, security for a Six comes when you have planned enough and feel ready. You are proud of your ability to plan for contingencies... constantly. With crisis mode as your modus operandi, so many uncertainties in caregiving—progressive aging or illness, unstable relationships, the ever-changing medical system—can any circumstance, person, or organization ever truly be trusted? Livingin a hyper-aroused adrenaline state is just as unrealistic as being totally unprepared. Caregiving is no time for living in an imagined world, especially one that breeds fear.

Six's concerns about what might happen leave her with a million questions. If you are a Six you may notice the positive, but in your quest for answers your mind generates negative possibilities, so your attention is focused on problems and problem-solving. Now more than ever it is critical to question your unhelpful imaginings.

The root cause of your predicament is that you look for certainty in an uncertain world, hoping that another person or situation will create the solid ground you are looking for. If you are fortunate to find that solid person, group, or cause, your loyalty knows no bounds. However, relying on externals to provide your security is, in itself, a vulnerable way to live. Better to cultivate your own self-confidence, self-reliance, and faith.

Sixes are the only type that is divided into two categories because they respond to their fears in two very different ways. Phobic Sixes tend to run from their fears, looking for someplace to hide. Counterphobic Sixes outwardly challenge their real or imagined fears and concerns, either confronting others with probing questions or challenging themselves by meeting their fears head on. Attacking the fear creates a surge of feeling more secure. These are the folks who jump out of airplanes to conquer heights, or take on caregiving with a fierce determination. Most Sixes are a bit of both, but some can be more extremely one or the other.

six's Positive Traits

More than any other type, you thrive in crisis situations. Problems? No problem! You have solutions, options, and strategic plans to target, change, or solve what is ailing. You provide in-home safety devices for your Loved One. You watch their ability to drive like a hawk. You have a list of emergency phone numbers by your Loved One's phone and programmed into your cell phone. Not all Sixes are this prepared, but you want to be!

Fortunately for those for whom you care, you are the protectors. You support the underdog and rally under stress, doing what is right to support equality and fairness. You value bonding and love your role as guardian. You are there to offer advice or help in any storm.

Generally you are a team player, liking cooperation and mutual support, so you are a marvelous contribution to a family support team. You try to keep the family together, thus proving yourself a worthy contributor. You are family-oriented and your definition of family can be extensive, embracing friends and groups.

As a dedicated observer of people's idiosyncrasies and motivations, Sixes often have a great sense of humor without whitewashing what's real. Good news/bad news—you see all angles.

You are a thorough researcher, another great strength in caregiving. The research may take a while but ultimately you make good decisions. You aren't fooled by appearances. You go for what is solid underneath. Better to be safe than sorry.

Positive caregiving traits of a Six include: Protectiveness

Loyalty and self-sacrifice

Being prepared, organized, and reliable Strategic planning and analysis

Being a team player

six's challenges

Your worry and anxiety can be contagious, eroding your family and Loved One's peace of mind, but caregiving can help you to learn how to create the security you have been seeking, which will help everyone.

Six's Most Challenging Traits during Caregiving: Worry, anxiety, and second guessing Projecting your fears onto others

Questioning others to reveal themselves, then hiding yourself Being passive-aggressive

Expecting others to make you secure Being critical, and black-or-white

Doubt - Though you are often solid as a rock, your inner questioning can cause you to vacillate on important decisions. Others can never be as consistent, reliable, or solid as you would like. People give as they can but not always what you expect. They may be dealing with their own feelings and confusion.

Over-control - Trying to control change may have anchored you in the past, but caregiving IS change and requires a different approach. Trying to muscle it into submission will be a major source of your stress if you don't find another way to navigate.

Self-generated Fear - A good deal of your fear and insecurity is self-created. When insecurity is mounting, your mind is likely the main culprit. Worst-case thinking doesn't protect you, it weakens you. Your over-active imagination undermines your effectiveness and your happiness.

six's opportunities for Personal Growth

You grow by not falling prey to your mind. You mind gives information and intuition but often exaggerates the fear aspects of situations. Trust your instinct more than the fear. Get feedback and focus on the positive. For Sixes to grow, take these steps:

Self-trust - One of your key lessons is to put more trust in yourself, demanding less reassurance from others. You want solidity and consistency but the only true solidity is within yourself. Let go of your ideal of finding the perfect partner or teammate and your caregiving will be more flexible and realistic. Focus more on providing your own self- esteem, safety, compassion, and understanding. Be your own authority, trusting yourself to be your foundation.

Release of control - Caregiving offers you another key lesson, the release of control for the sake of growing resilience. By accepting each moment as it is, moving with life while handling the details, you can work with your care process while adapting to change.

Mind-management - Mind control has been, for you, a key path toward security. Shift your focus so that your imagination can be an equally valuable ally. When you feel fearful, redirect your attention to activities or interests. Consciously focus on positive things that happen. Say affirmations. Scrutinize yourself with the same spotlight that you shine at others so that you know your own fears, insecurities, and doubts and put them in their place. Then balance your work with play, adventure, tolerance for others' independent processes, and greater acceptance of change.

Trust yourself. People don't always have answers for you, and that includes authority figures. Listen to your own desires and intuition. Gather the research and believe in your own ability to make decisions. Learn from those who have experience, but don't look to them as having all the answers.

Bring attention inside - If your attention is outside, scanning for problems, you forget to come inside yourself and notice that you actually might be feeling secure in yourself. Throughout the day, bring the attention back to yourself and you may feel better.

Don't look for trouble - You tend to be on the lookout for safety and security concerns, but when all is running smoothly, don't look over

your shoulder for problems. Sometimes you feel more relaxed when there are issues at hand. Trust that you can enjoy the quiet, comfortable, or fun periods with nothing dangling over your head. Don't create problems.

Question if your fear is real - You can be confused, because adrenaline still kicks in, even when dangers are only imagined. Get feedback from others about what is real to them. Of course, trust your intuition and evidence, but don't assume you always understand others' motivations or intentions. Don't jump to conclusions. Think the best, as well as the worst. Recall times in your life where you jumped to conclusions and made situations worse!

Ask fewer questions and reveal yourself more - That is hard to do, as you tend to ask a million questions to gather as much information as possible to be prepared for all eventualities. Sometimes this is hard on others, and they feel barraged by probes or questions that ask too much. Reveal as much about yourself as you want others to reveal about themselves! Answer questions and talk about yourself, before you question.

Assume the best - Let's up the ante. Look for the best in every situation or at least the part that is good. Don't throw out the whole thing because of a few concerns or flaws. Enjoy people for what they can be and don't expect the impossible.

Make decisions - Sometimes you wait until forever to make decisions, because you feel sure, then unsure, then sure, then unsure. Decide! Some doubt and insecurity are normal. You will seldom be 100 percent sure about anything. Learn as you go along and correct along the way. Let go of some of the what-ifs. Catch yourself each time you use that language.

Let go of the past - You can hang on to past mistrusts of others. If someone apologizes and learns a lesson, let it go. The past is gone. Learn from it, but don't dwell on it. Choose more wisely in the future, if necessary. We all make mistakes. Everyone, including you, sometimes tells white lies or withholds. Be more forgiving. Look at what does work and have a full memory for everything, not just the bad.

Release anxiety - You need to let go of some of your anxiety. It is stressful to overly plan, over prepare, and imagine the worst. Do some relaxation techniques, such as breathing, visualization, yoga, meditation,

or exercise. Take up some hobbies and get back into your body, when your head is working overtime. Do some creative activities or use your head to figure out puzzles or word games.

six's Heart, soul and Mind

As one of the types that is most aware of their inner state, your inner world is the source of both your problems and your peace. Your stumbling blocks are not caused by the concrete challenges of caregiving, they are caused by the way you interpret what is happening.

sixes in Relationships

Relationships are essential for Sixes. You are a trustworthy partner and friend, and feel so responsible that it can be hard to understand others' lack of accountability. How can she promise something and not do it? Why isn't he totally honest with me? Don't I deserve honesty? Questions like this abound. But are you as forthcoming as you want others to be?

You like relationships, yet being too close brings up fear. You are concerned if you share too much, or if they don't share as much as you. You find it hard when others have values and ideas that are different from yours. If they are honest with stating those differences, it helps.

You are psychologically sophisticated. You tune in to motivations, and what is happening below the surface. You are a sleuth—you look for clues and feel more secure when you can figure people out. But sometimes, in your need for security and exact explanations, you can seem intrusive. Your questions can verge on being challenging, rather than caring or curious. Since you tend to be more other-focused, maybe you need to take care of yourself more and be less concerned about others' motivations.

You are willing to sacrifice in a good relationship. You understand crises and challenges and can stay resolved and committed during difficult times. Having a problem to fix is a catalyst for your action and connection, but it is also just as important to be steady and relaxed during times of ease and solidity. Don't fill your mind with potential problems. Enjoy life and be comforted for now.

Relationship Advice for Sixes:

Consider revealing your emotions and insecurities in your key relationships. You expect honesty from others, so share yourself personally, lest others feel rejected. Communicate before pulling back in order to reflect.

Practice sharing your process as it is happening, rather than merely revealing your conclusions. Tell others when you are caught off guard by sudden emotions or changed plans require instant response.

Make requests of others that will let you prepare for emotional interactions. Ask them to explain what they're feeling and to make their expectations clear, as you show your interest in their process. Tell them that you may need to explore feelings without having to over-define them.

How Sixes Think

Sixes are always planning, preparing for future "what ifs." You spend time imagining about your Loved One's health and what could happen. You have fearful, angry thoughts about unfairness and injustice. Occasionally you think about positive things too.

Things Sixes think about:

I want to predict what might happen. What did he mean by that?

There's a difference between what you say and what you do! I wish I could understand this.

Why did she do it differently this time?

Sixes wish they could say:

I feel secure. I'll be ready for whatever comes. I'll ask but without alarm.

People don't always do what they say, but then neither do I. Sometimes I change my mind.

I don't understand it, but that's fine. It'll make sense in time.

How Sixes Make Decisions

You tie with Nines for being the most reluctant decision makers. Ambivalence is the norm; certainty-doubt-certainty-doubt-certainty- doubt. Of course caregiving decisions can feel risky but so is not making them. Do your research, and then take informed steps. If you can, make some test decisions that have lesser consequences. You'll learn, either way.

Notice when your indecisiveness reflects worst-case scenario thinking, and when actual circumstances, thank God, aren't as bad as your mind may imagine. It is normal to have some doubt but be sure to think of best-case scenarios too. And when you feel fed up with procrastination, beware of making hasty or rash major decisions.

Six's Spiritual Side

Sixes' spirituality is rooted in trusting group consciousness and believing what is tried and true. You tend to believe in God as a protector and believe we must bond together in groups and communities to survive and grow. You appreciate the sacrifices others have made for your well-being.

You see the bad and need to believe in the good while hoping for a higher power. You need faith to see that there is something more reliable than your fears, dangers, and concerns - faith in life itself, authorities who really care, people motivated to do good. Your hope is that other people are also motivated by higher traits and qualities.

Sixes are loyal members of the congregation, as well as questioners of the truth. Is the minister trustworthy? What are the real motivations of committee members? Are we promoting the right things? Are people really committed and really honest about what they are thinking? You're willing to work through the challenges to build more trust and bonding. You are the sentinels for security for yourself and others.

As some sixes doubt, question everything and are skeptical, you will find in some sixes a down to earth focus without much spirituality, though being down to earth often draws a trust in the earth and physical reality. 6s have hope though when they see genuiousness, generosity, sacrifice and honesty in others.

Making the Most of Being a Six

Sixes Stress Type, Growth Type, and Wings can be a great comfort to the Six by moderating her fears, offering growth opportunities, and lightening up her demeanor.

Six's Stress Type - The Achieving Three ☐

Growth Type - The Peaceful Nine

When under stress, the Six, with a Stress Type of the Achieving Three, revs up for action and completion without first getting centered. You get into action, anxiously doing things without reference to the goal. You also may be image/success oriented in order to protect yourself from seeming insecure. Better to spend some time alone to self-connect, then figure out what to do, and then finally act with less anxiety. A highly useful ally for a caregiver is her intuition. Get some feedback if necessary, but don't let others decide for you. Go to the high side of Three- - clarify goals, take action steps, and then picture the positive happening.

The Growth Type for Six is Nine, the Peaceful Caregiver. Nines know how to relax, tend to be positive, and imagine people and life being nice, rather than dangerous. What a gift these traits can be during caregiving! Nines rest, take breaks, and enjoy the simple things in life, exactly what the doctor ordered for Sixes who generally need to slow down. All of Nine's qualities are balance points for the Six during this stressful time.

Sixes see the hard side of caregiving a bit too much, while Nines avoid the bad. Find the balance in between where you see the good and the bad, and hold both in mind at the same time. You'll walk the path of your commitment with more grace and ease.

Six's Wings, The Knowledgeable Five & The Playful Seven

While Six's Five wing intensifies her questioning and analyzing, the Seven wing softens the Six, bringing a welcome breath of lightness and humor.

A Six with a strong Five wing holds on to what she believes in and analyzes things to death! You are a systems person and a thorough researcher. You're a bit serious, even cynical, and yet you know what you're talking about. You try to create solidity but are always questioning

and seeing the cracks in the granite. And there are so many cracks in every system! You defend what you believe in. You tend to be traditional, though you can also challenge traditions and start new traditions. Downside? The caregiver's common stumbling block—you can get too isolated, not trusting feedback from others. You can be a bit too much in your head and theoretical, though you can also be brilliant!

Six with a Seven wing is more relationship oriented, and lighter in tone, so welcome when caregiving. You like jokes, self-deprecating humor, and are more extroverted. Liking a bit of fun, you're a natural comedian, making fun of your own insecurity. Downside? Sometimes it is hard to distinguish whether you are secure or insecure. Let yourself reveal your insecurities and let your family and buddies help.

Six's Degrees of Balance

Well-balanced Sixes are wonderful. You question, but not too much. You realize that caregiving, like life, is complex and mostly happens in the gray area between black and white. You need no more definition from others than from yourself. You are protective, empathic, caring, and allow people their individuality. You work hard for the causes you believe in. You fight for the underdog and justice and you understand psychological dynamics. You are not easily fooled, yet you also focus on and remember what is good. You make an excellent Elders' advocate in the nursing home or hospital.

Average Sixes worry, focusing too much on fear, and miss out on tending to what is good. There is always some good, even in the most trying of circumstances. Relationships are important but you can expect too much from people who have their own problems. You look for security

177

outside yourself, and need to focus more on providing it for yourself. You want others to be committed to you or as committed as you are to them. Make sure you are committed yourself, providing what your Loved One really needs, not what you think they need. Make sure you can let in the good that builds a feeling of security. Trust yourself about how to be in the moment.

Out-of-balance Sixes can be paranoid, living in worst case as a norm, and can't trust the good. Everyone is suspect and the "weather" can turn at any moment. Everything is an emergency. Your adrenaline is affecting

your health, your Loved One's health, and that of the family. Some of this can be helped by developing a memory for what is positive, but be honest with yourself. If your caregiving style is doing more damage than good, look for ways to bring in others to help balance your approach.

Chapter 17: Type Four Personality

TYPE FOUR (individualist and romantic) - As an individualist, a Type Four personality wants to define his or her own unique identity and also be significant rather than being a mere passer-by. They may struggle with adapting to an environment where human behaviour is regulated by laid-down rules. As a romantic, a Type Four is a supportive, passionate and empathetic being. They primarily derive their sense of self-worth from their relationships.

The characteristics of Type Fours are as follows -

• Individuals with Type Four personality trait are sensitive to what others are going through and are willing to offer support in any way they can. These individuals can spot things that others ignore and that is why they have a special ability to dissect a problem and detect its root causes. They love to help others even when there are no immediate benefits or gains. They consider the inputs to relationships as currencies that can be traded to get whatever they want even there are no returns at present.

• These Type Four personality individuals long for something which they may no longer value as much as they should when they have it. Their spouses may have a hard time appreciating this side of them because they may be difficult to please. It is, therefore, better to delay their gratification when relating with them.

• Type Fours have a tendency to blame themselves for their misfortunes even when other factors are to blame. They always feel there is something they could have done to change the situation they find themselves in. Having an internal locus of control could also enable them to fix certain issues in their lives without seeking the help of others.

• Type Fours have a deep sense of respect for celebrities and persons in authority who appear to have something special about them. This is the main reason they can be drawn to odd personalities like radical feminists, eccentric rock stars, rebel leaders, magicians, survivalists and so on and so forth. Without realising it, they may see such persons as role models and in some extreme cases, as idols.

● Type Fours draw their energies from others and rely on how they are perceived. by or what they can contribute to other people and being part of the emotional group, their feelings and those of close friends matter to them. They have a small inner circle of like-minded individuals who mean a lot to them. Outside this inner circle, they might not pay much attention to what the world out there thinks or feels about them.

● Type Fours are comfortable living an eccentric life and they often reflect this kind of lifestyle in their daily habits. They may be vegetarian or maintain the use of the same house or car for many years as long as it is meeting their needs. They can be very profound in their worldview and approach to life. It is not uncommon to find a Type Four asking questions about the meaning and origins of life. Being philosophical can get their energy levels up when discussing or arguing about such deep life issues.

• Their worldviews, more often than not, are unconventional and this bothers them very little. They feel there are always going to be people out there who share their views on the same subject or issue. They could spend the rest of their lives campaigning for the promotion of animal rights or the financial inclusion of the less privileged in society or even the protection of gay rights in the communities where they live and work.

• Type Fours have a penchant for daydreaming about the future or getting mentally stuck in the past. Once they get a clear picture of what ought to be (whether in their personal lives, family, organization or nation), they could begin to imagine it coming into existence and this process can take place for years without people around them getting a hint about it. The same process may take place as regards the past as they could be trying to rewrite the scripts of the past in their minds.

Below are the examples of renowned 'Type Four' personalities in human history -

● FRANCIS BACON - An English philosopher, statesman, and scientist who served as both the attorney general and Lord Chancellor of England. He is referred to as the father of empiricism because his works were influential in the development of the scientific method during the scientific revolution. As a Type Four, he stated that he had three goals: to uncover the truth, serve his country and to serve the church. He sought to further these ends by seeking a prestigious post. According to his personal secretary and chaplain, Francis Bacon was always tender-hearted, was free from malice, did not revenge or defame any man.

● MARLON BRANDO - An American actor and film director who had a considerable cultural influence on the movie industry in the 20th century. He made a number of award-winning appearances in popular movies over the course of three decades and was an activist for different causes including the civil rights movement. His Type Four personality may have been reinforced in his childhood which was characterized by a lack of love and affection from his father who had a habit of telling him that he could not do anything right and would not amount to anything. So he grew up wanting to feel special and loved.

- MICHAEL JACKSON - An American singer and dancer often referred to as the King of Pop. As one of the most popular entertainers in the world and one of the best-selling music artists of all time, his contribution to music, fashion, and dance along with his publicized personal life made him a global figure in popular culture for over four decades. His Type Four personality was reinforced by a troubled childhood which he considers non-existent. Michael Jackson stated that he was physically and emotionally abused during incessant rehearsals. Though he credited his father's strict discipline with playing a huge role in his career. His deep dissatisfaction with his appearance and his tendency to remain hyper-compliant and to remain childlike in adulthood are consistent with the effects of the maltreatment he endured as a child.

- PRINCE CHARLES OF WALES - The eldest child of Queen Elizabeth II and the heir apparent to the British throne. He has been the Duke of Cornwall and Duke of Rothesay since 1952 and is the oldest and longest-serving heir apparent in British history. Prince Charles broke a number of royal traditions in his quest to be different. He was the first heir apparent to be educated within the four walls of a school rather than being schooled by a private tutor. Also, he chose to proceed to the university rather than join the British Armed Forces immediately after high school, a break away from the norm in British royalty.

• VINCENT VAN GOGH - A Dutch painter who is among the most famous and influential figures in the history of western art. In just over a decade, he created about 2,100 works of art including 860 oil paintings, most of them in the last two years of his life. His work included landscapes, still- life portraits and self-portraits characterized by bold colors and expressive brushwork that contributed to the foundations of modern art. Vincent Van Gogh was a classical Type Four. He was unsuccessful during his lifetime and was considered a madman and a failure. He became famous after his suicide and exists in the public imagination as the quintessential misunderstood genius and artist.

• NICHOLAS CAGE - An American actor, director, and producer who has received awards for his writing and acting prowess. These awards include an Academy Award, Golden Globe Award, and a Screen Actors Guild Award. As a Type Four, he chooses to do things his own way. Without realizing it at the initial stage of his career, he managed to develop his own acting style which he referred to as 'Nouveau Shamanic.' He is known to be attracted to grotesque characters and is celebrated for his wild and unhinged approach to them. He has been described as the only actor since Marlon Brando that has actually done anything new with the art of movie-acting, crediting him for taking film audiences away from an obsession with naturalism into a kind of presentation style that was popular with the troubadours. As a young boy, Michelangelo was sent to study grammar in Florence but he showed no interest in schooling, preferring to copy paintings from churches and seek the company of other painters.

● MICHELANGELO - An Italian sculptor, painter, architect, and poet who exerted an unparalleled influence on the development of the western art. He has been described as one of the greatest artists of all time and also considered as the archetypal Renaissance man. As the best-documented artist of the 16th century, some of his works of painting, sculpture, and architecture rank among the most famous in existence. He lived a very frugal life and wanted to do virtually everything in moderation, regardless of the wealth or resources at his disposal. He was by nature a solitary and melancholy person who liked to withdraw himself from the company of men.

- EDGAR ALLAN POE - An American writer, editor and literary critic who is best known for his poetry and short stories. His works influenced literature in the United States and around the world and continue to appear throughout popular culture in literature, music, films, and television. He also played pivotal roles in the development of literary genres like detective fiction and science fiction. As a foster child, he was alternately spoiled and aggressively disciplined by his father. This may have caused the Type Four trait to be strengthened years later. He is reputed as the first well-known American writer who attempted to earn a living from writing alone.

The typical roles played by Type Fours include -

● THE MAVERICK - A typical Four personality is an independent thinker who is never afraid to swim against the tide. When they are confronted with an issue, they think clearly and logically before taking sides, if they even do so at all. Where most people belong to one political party or the other, they may choose not to align with any of them and prefer to take a stand based on political orientations or leanings.

● THE OUTSIDER - Type Fours do not mind separating themselves from a group in a psychological sense if they feel the values and orientation of the group does not match theirs. They would not normally feign alignment or unity just to please an individual or group. Their views on issues matter so much to them.

● THE MISFIT - Type Fours may represent the odd guy or lady in a group especially when they are lacking in compliance with stated rules and norms. When taken to the extreme in negative terms, they could become a serious headache in society as they may commit crimes that they justify in their own minds.

- THE CONNOISSEUR - A Type Four personality may develop his abilities and faculties to very high levels that makes them an expert in a particular field of interest. They concentrate all their energies on mastering a particular task or discipline and van easily do what others may find relatively difficult to accomplish.

- THE BOHEMIAN - A Bohemian is usually an intellectual or artist who is living an unconventional lifestyle and you would not find a better fit than that of a Type Four personality. It doesn't matter whether they win a Nobel Prize for science or literature, they are wholly devoted to their work and such work often has its roots in how they generally see life.

- THE POET IN THE GARRET - A garret is a section of a house that is situated under the roof or attic. Being a poet in the garret, Type Fours like to work alone rather than in teams. They find their strength in solitude as it helps to unlock their genius and creativity. Working in a tranquil environment helps them to stay productive.

• THE SELF-DESTRUCTIVE GENIUS - When taken to an extreme, they could begin to hallucinate and create illusory perceptions about reality. Therefore, their ideas or outputs may be farther away from reality and may not be useful or applicable. They sometimes need a constant reality check and the inputs of others to produce desirable results.

• THE SPURNED LOVER - Type Fours may not care about the attention and opinions of everyone but those of the few they like to mean a lot to them. And when those few persons do not give attention or disapprove of their viewpoints, it can be very demoralizing to them. Being spurned may cause them to feel depressed or moody.

• THE ARISTOCRAT - Type Fours are capable of living a well-ordered life that creates an aura of nobility around them. They have been known to deny themselves of pleasure just to achieve this. Self-discipline comes to them naturally and once locked in on a habit or routine, find it very difficult to change it.

● THE LONER - Type Fours may not be particularly anti-social but alone time means a lot to them. They would do all they can to spend some time alone no matter how busy a schedule they have. Being alone could also translate spending time with members of the inner circle with whom they feel most comfortable.

Type Fours are people with a deep desire to be different in every area of their lives - thinking, appearance, views, habits. They do not like to conform or fit into the box unconsciously created by society. Being distinctive from others give them a sense of satisfaction and they connect better with a few individuals within the group rather than the entire group. They may not abide by specified rules and regulations but can make vital contributions in terms of originality and creativity. On the positive side, they can be supportive, intuitive, refined, compassionate and creative. On the negative side, they can stubborn, guilt-ridden, moralistic, withdrawn and self-conscious.

Chapter 18: Type 5 And 6 Characteristics

Synopsis

An investigator is an analyzer of information and the best course of action. They are also a type of thinker who likes to take a back seat, observe the situation, make all the analytical considerations for the best options and comes back after a full analysis of the situation is done.

A type six is a mixed bag of fear versus courage, loyalty versus skepticism and the guardian angel or the rebel. They are the person who is epitomized by the famous song "Stand by me".

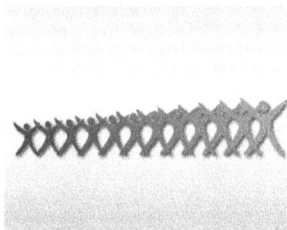

Type 5 Characteristics - Observer, Investigator, Thinker, Sage or Voyeur

They typically do not share their emotional state with others as they hold back often finding security in their minds where they can withdraw and strategize, only to emerge later with full confidence! You can always count on them to give intelligent answers, and when they are interested in something, they tend to become really well read and knowledgeable in that area.

They are also a little shy but more independent (or reluctant to accept help) preferring to get things done on their own even when other people are more than willing to give help. They tend not to share anything much especially when their primary fixation of stinginess is manifested.

Their holy idea is Omniscience. They will not stop until they know and understand everything their finite minds can hold. Their greatest fear is uselessness or helplessness. They, like the type threes also desire to be highly competent.

They desire to be competent in all tasks. Because they are the big brains of the group, they are often looked upon as the one with all the answers and the best course of action.

Their biggest temptation is over thinking. Because of their introverted, analytical nature, they tend to hold back, not taking action.

Their greatest vice is avarice – because of their desire to know and have everything coupled with their stingy nature, they often fall into this problem of wanting everything for themselves.

However, the type ones are at their best when they learn to detach themselves and live free.

Type fives with a wing of four and wins of six have one strong distinction – art and science. Wing fours combine intellectual and emotional imagination. Those with wings of sixes are technically competent and are very good at finding the distinctions in what's working and what's missing.

Type 6 Characteristics - Loyal Person, Devil's Advocate, Skeptic, Guardian or Rebel

The day they build solid trust with someone, they will stick by them all the way until the end. They are a very unique type of people when it comes to trust because they tend to trust people almost as much as they distrust people at the same time. These people are always constantly looking for something or someone to believe in deeply – once the people they believe in have 'earned their trust', they will be loyal till death. They tend to react to fear in one or two ways (especially when their primary fixation of cowardice is manifested) either by embracing the fear head one (counter-phobic six) or avoiding it at all costs (phobic six).

It's no surprise that their holy idea is faith. They always believe that in spite of their fears and uncertainties, something good always lie around the corner.

Their greatest fear is isolation and vulnerability. They can't live without a strong support system and they can't stand being abandoned.

They desire safety above all else. They are skeptics by nature and will question everything and test everything until it breaks but deep down inside, they wish to know that everything will be okay.

Their biggest temptation is suspiciousness which leads to them questioning motives and relationships can become very taxing.

Their greatest vice fear as they are generally fearful of many things and they relate their lives, their stresses and their motivations towards or away from their fears.

However, the type ones are at their best when they develop the courage to face their   fears.
Type sixes with a wing of give are often more introverted and intellectual. They can become very strong critics. The other wings are the types that appear more overtly nervous. They can also falsely

accuse others without realizing it. They are also more charming and sociable.

Conclusion

The first step towards self-transformation is self-discovery. Without self-discovery, we are doomed to keep on repeating and following our old patterns of behavior unconsciously. And as long as we keep this cycle going on and on, we will keep getting the results of the past.

Albert Einstein said, "The definition of insanity is doing the same things over and over again, but expecting different results." If we keep living our past, we will keep getting the results of the past in the present. To change our lives for the better, we have to discover the real problem, develop the plan and put in the action to change.

"Problems cannot be solved by the level of awareness that created them," says Albert Einstein. Could it be that many people never discover their personality by themselves without any special tool? Our personality was formed during the formative stages of life and was made concrete as we pass through life.

While many of us still have formidable strengths, the weakness of our character seems to slow and delay our progress in life. Thanks to the

Enneagram that provides a deep insight into our personality, shows us what went wrong, where the problem lies with our personality, and what is missing in the picture.

When you perform the Enneagram test for the first time and you find your type and wings, you will discover something more than yourself like never before. The Enneagram reveals the unconscious motivations, fears, and desires that drive your everyday actions. You identify your strengthens and weaknesses, and finally know your type.

While knowing your Enneagram type is very important. Taking a closer look at your wing type and analyzing the role it plays in your life is crucial. How are the wing types affecting your everyday life?

How does the combined impact of your core and wing-type affect and influence your life?

The Enneagram report is much more revealing. Get the full details about your personality. When you do, don't stop there. The next step is to commit to a personal development and growth program that will move you on the road to the essence. The main goal of the Enneagram is to discover where you fell from essence and then work back to that level. What you want to do is to become the best version of yourself.

And that means working on yourself and transforming your unholy desires to the holy desires. It means converting your vices into virtues by doing the "inner work" of transformation that Ichazo talked about when he first introduced the Enneagram. It is only by discovering our type and doing the inner work that we get to the real essence.

We get closer to the real essence when we discover our unhealthy type and then work through the development stages to make it healthy. The fact is that your unhealthy type negatively affects all aspects of your life: career, finance, marriage, family, organization and everything you do.

Therefore, nothing changes in your life until you transform your personality. The better you get with your personality; the better life gets for you. Just like what Jim Rohn said, "If you change yourself, everything will change for you." When you commit to discovering and developing your personality, your life will transform completely.

According to the Enneagram, there are three centers of intelligence: the head, heart, and body. Our thinking, feeling, and actions influence what we do and affect our personality over time. Whereas in the past, you have been unconsciously programmed by society and the external environment to live in a certain way, you can take complete charge over your centers of intelligence and take control of your life.

Sometimes the journey to a healthy type can be hard and challenging. That means getting a credible Enneagram coach or therapist to help you do the "inner work" to develop yourself. The right Enneagram will analyze your current condition, map out a personal development plan and then help you grow your personality over a period of time.

If you dedicate to learning about the Enneagram, discovering your enneatype and working steadily on growing yourself with the help of an Enneagram coach/therapist, the compound effect will be exhilarating. You'll be amazed at how you will develop your personality over a period of time.

The compound effect will make a profound difference in marriage, career, relationship, family, finances, and social life. People all around you will realize that you are making positive changes in your life that are constantly reflecting in your life. You will find yourself manifesting, exhibiting and showing more of the qualities of the divine nature of true essence.

www.ingramcontent.com/pod-product-compliance
Lightning Source LLC
Chambersburg PA
CBHW062131020426
42335CB00013B/1178